PANZER I
VS
T-26

Spanish Civil War 1936–39

JACEK ZABIELSKI

OSPREY PUBLISHING
Bloomsbury Publishing Plc
Kemp House, Chawley Park, Cumnor Hill, Oxford OX2 9PH, UK
Bloomsbury Publishing Ireland Limited,
29 Earlsfort Terrace, Dublin 2, D02 AY28, Ireland
Bloomsbury Publishing Inc.
1359 Broadway, 12th Floor, New York, NY 10018, USA
E-mail: info@ospreypublishing.com
www.ospreypublishing.com

OSPREY is a trademark of Osprey Publishing Ltd

First published in Great Britain in 2026

ISBN: PB 9781472873620; eBook 9781472873637;
ePDF 9781472873606; XML 9781472873613

26 27 28 29 30   10 9 8 7 6 5 4 3 2 1

Maps by bounford.com
Index by Angela Hall
Typeset by Lumina Datamatics Ltd
Printed by Repro India Ltd.

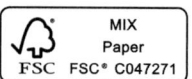

FSC FSC® C047271
MIX
Paper

Osprey Publishing supports the Woodland Trust, the UK's leading woodland
conservation charity.

To find out more about our authors and books visit
www.ospreypublishing.com. Here you will find extracts, author interviews,
details of forthcoming events and the option to sign up for our newsletter.

For product safety related questions contact productsafety@bloomsbury.com

Photo credits
ACKM – Archive of the Soviet Peace Committee (*Arkhiv Sovetskovo Komiteta Mira*)
BDH – Biblioteca Digital Hispánica
BNE – Biblioteca Nacional España
CMVS - Central Military Archive of the Russian Federation (Центральный военный архив России)
NAC – National Digital Archives (Narodowe Archiwum Cyfrowe)
RGAKFD – Russian State Archive of the Armed Forces of the Russian Federation (Российский государственный архив Вооруженных сил Российской Федерации)

Title-page photograph: Only four modified PzKpfw I Breda tanks were
produced, each armed with a 2cm anti-aircraft gun, with one tank assigned to
each Panzer company. (Author's Collection)

CONTENTS

INTRODUCTION

Following the turmoil of the February and October revolutions of 1917 and the subsequent Civil War of 1917–22, the Soviet Union's leadership concluded that the country needed a strong, modern army to defend itself against potential foreign invasions and internal dissent. To achieve this goal, the country began developing its tank industry, leading to the establishment of numerous new factories and nearly 100 ancillary tank-parts suppliers during the first two five-year plans (1928–37). Initially, Soviet factories produced copies of the French Renault FT light tank, followed in 1926 by the Soviet T-18 light tank, a modestly improved version of the Renault FT. Shortly thereafter, the T-19 light tank was introduced, a Soviet derivative of the French Renault NC light tank.

In 1926, under the terms of a secret agreement between Germany and the Soviet Union, a German facility codenamed Panzertruppenschule Kama was established near Kazan, in Soviet territory. This facility was intended as a testing and training site for German tank prototypes, away from the eyes of Britain and France, and outside the constraints of the Versailles Treaty of 1919. In exchange, the Soviet Union was to receive valuable engineering and manufacturing expertise for its own armour programme, although the Soviet leadership remained cautious about too much collaboration, considering their old enemy (Germany) was funding and controlling the operation. The German tank prototypes tested in the Soviet Union were disappointing for both sides, however, as neither met the assumed specifications, thus limiting the technological benefits for the Soviet side. Despite this, Soviet–German cooperation continued until 1933, when it ended after Adolf Hitler came to power.

By the end of the 1920s, it became clear that the only rapid way to accelerate the mechanization of the Red Army was through acquiring licensed production rights for new tank models. In 1929, the *Revolyutsionny Voyenny Sovyet* (Revolutionary Military

Council) established a special tank commission to visit European and American arms manufacturers in search of new tank designs. During a visit to the British Vickers-Armstrong Elswick Works in Newcastle upon Tyne in 1929, the Soviets signed a contract to produce 15 Vickers 6-Ton (aka Mark E) Type A light tanks armed with twin .303in Vickers machine-gun turrets. The 6-Ton, lightly armoured with a maximum thickness of 13mm, offered good cross-country mobility compared to World War I tanks. Although the British Army rejected the design, finding the suspension insufficiently robust, the Soviets chose to mass-produce the model as the T-26 light tank.

Starting in 1932, the first of the Red Army's mechanized corps were formed. Each corps consisted of two mechanized brigades (each with three tank battalions of 31 tanks per battalion) and one motorized brigade (with three battalions). By 1 May 1933, the Red Army had two mechanized corps and six tank brigades as part of its strategic reserves, using BT light tanks for cavalry and T-26s for infantry. By 1933, mixed platoons in mechanized brigades – consisting of one single-turret and two twin-turret T-26s – became the standard. By early 1935, tank battalions in infantry divisions were organized into three companies, each equipped with 15 T-26s.

With the mass development of the tank force, Soviet military doctrine began to be shaped by Marshal Mikhail N. Tukhachevsky, whose doctrine emphasized the mass

A first-series twin-turret T-26 mod. 1931. The only difference between the early T-26s and the British Vickers Mark E Type A light tank was that the Soviet turrets were adapted to mount DT light machine guns, and the embrasures were rectangular, not round. Starting in the autumn of 1931, T-26s of the so-called second series were equipped with higher turrets featuring a vision port. (ACKM)

Three of the 20 makeshift Krupp tanks were employed during the Münster manoeuvres in August 1935. (Author's Collection)

The T-26 mod. 1933 was known as the *radiyniy tank* ('radio tank'). (Author's Collection)

deployment of tanks in close cooperation with artillery and the air force. His plan envisaged motorized infantry accompanying the tanks, enabling them to annihilate the enemy on their own territory in a mobile, fast-paced war. Command structures, training and armament were all designed to support this vision.

By 1934, the Soviet Union's tank force had already become the largest in the world, while Germany's tank force was still in its infancy. Although new tank models were still under development, the theoretical speculations of German armoured specialists began to gain more significance. On 1 April 1931, Oberst Oswald Lutz was promoted to *Generalmajor* and appointed Inspector of Motor Transport Troops. Six months later, Oberstleutnant Heinz Guderian became Lutz's chief of staff, both of them being strong advocates for tank forces. When Hitler came to power in January 1933, he appointed General der Infanterie Werner von Blomberg as Germany's Minister of War and Generalmajor Walter von Reichenau as chief of the Ministerial Office; both officers supported tank development. That same year, during an exercise at the German Army ordnance testing centre at Kummersdorf, Guderian demonstrated to Hitler a motorcycle platoon and anti-tank guns alongside a new light tank, later designated the PzKpfw I, inspired by British Carden-Loyd tankettes. The Führer was deeply impressed, and Guderian became Germany's leading proponent of mechanized troops.

The early, secret development of the German tank force was based on just two *Kraftfahrlehrkommando* (tank-training units), designated Zossen and Ohrdruf. These were initially equipped with unarmed tracked vehicles, formally classified as light agricultural tractors to disguise the fact that Germany was developing armoured fighting vehicles. It was not until March 1935, after Hitler rejected the restrictions of the Versailles Treaty and reintroduced compulsory military service, that information about the existence of Germany's new armoured units was officially disclosed. Tank production was then given top priority in the German rearmament programme. A few months later, on 15 October 1935, the first of three Panzer divisions was established, which consisted of two Panzer regiments with two battalions each, totalling over 250 light tanks. These tanks were still no match for the French, British and Soviet tanks of that era, however.

CHRONOLOGY

1930

October The Soviet Union receives the first of 15 Vickers Mark E Type A light tanks, the basis of the T-26 light-tank design.

1931

December The Red Army takes delivery of the first 100 T-26s.

1933

July The first five German *Kleintraktoren* with machine-gun turrets are completed.

November Generalmajor Oswald Lutz organizes Germany's first tank-training unit, Kraftfahrlehrkommando Zossen.

December The single-turret, gun-armed T-26 variant enters production.

1936

February The Frente Popular (Popular Front) narrowly wins the Spanish general election.

17 July A military uprising against the Spanish Republic begins in Morocco.

Ex-Republican T-26 mod. 1935s captured by Nationalist forces were used in the Spanish Legion's tank battalion. By the end of the Spanish Civil War, nearly 100 captured T-26s had been deployed in combat, assisting the PzKpfw I-equipped units. (Author's Collection)

27 July	German and Italian aircraft begin airlifting the *Ejército de África* (Army of Africa; aka Army of Spanish Morocco) from Morocco to southern Spain.
August	Production of the improved PzKpfw I Ausf B light tank begins in Germany.
October	The first shipment of T-26s for the Spanish Republican Army is sent from the Soviet Union aboard the cargo ship SS *Komsomol*.
November	Panzergruppe Drohne is deployed to Spain.
8 November	The battle of Madrid begins, involving T-26s and PzKpfw Is.

A PzKpfw I of the 5th Panzer Company in March 1938, during the 'March to the Sea' campaign. (Author's Collection)

1937

March	T-26s assist Republican forces during the battle of Guadalajara, contributing to the destruction of Italy's *Corpo Truppe Volontarie* (Corps of Voluntary Troops).
July	The unsuccessful Republican offensive at Brunete involves more than 100 T-26s.

1938

January	Start of the last major campaign around Teruel, in which Soviet tank crews participate.
14 April	Nationalist forces reach the Mediterranean at Vinaroz, splitting the Second Spanish Republic (1931–39) in two.
25 July	Republican forces cross the Ebro River in a major, unsuccessful offensive.

1939

March	The 'March to the Sea' begins, becoming the most successful Nationalist operation by mechanized forces, including PzKpfw Is, in the entire Spanish Civil War.
13 March	The last shipment of Soviet T-26s for the Republican Army.
28 March	Nationalist forces enter Madrid while General Francisco Franco announces the end of the Spanish Civil War.
11 May	Soviet forces including T-26s fight Japanese forces in Mongolia.
12 August	The Soviet Union signs a non-aggression pact with Germany.
1 September	German forces including PzKpfw Is invade Poland.
17 September	Soviet forces including T-26s invade Poland.
30 November	Soviet forces including T-26s invade Finland.

1940

9 April	German forces including PzKpfw Is invade Denmark and Norway.
10 May	German forces including PzKpfw Is invade France and the Low Countries.
15 June	Soviet forces including T-26s occupy Estonia, Latvia and Lithuania.
28 June	Soviet forces including T-26s invade Bessarabia.

1941

22 June	Operation *Barbarossa*, the Axis invasion of the Soviet Union, begins, with roughly 300 PzKpfw Is involved; the Red Army fields more than 3,000 T-26s.

DESIGN AND DEVELOPMENT

T-26

In 1929, a contract was signed between the British firm Vickers-Armstrong and the *Upravleniye Motorizatzii I Mekhanizatzii Raboche-krestyanskaya Krasnaya Armiya* (UMM RKKA: Directorate of Mechanization and Motorization of the Red Army) for the production and delivery of 15 Vickers Mark E Type A light tanks to the Soviet Union. The tanks were delivered to the Soviet Union between October 1930 and July 1931. Each cost the Soviet Union 42,000 rubles (at 1931 prices); the domestically produced T-19 cost over 96,000 rubles. The imported tanks were also simpler to manufacture and maintain and had better mobility than the T-19.

Intended to serve as the standard support tank for combined-arms units and the Red Army's strategic reserves, the British tanks were accepted into Red Army service on 13 February 1931, and given the designation T-26. Despite their thin armour, which at the time was not considered a significant drawback (in the late 1920s, no army had specialized anti-tank guns or developed anti-tank defence systems), the T-26s proved well-suited for its role as a light infantry-support tank.

Initial production of the T-26 was planned for the newly built Chelyabinsk Tractor Plant, followed by the Stalingrad Tractor Plant then under construction, which was to include a workshop capable of producing up to 10,000 tanks annually in wartime.

Twin-turreted T-26s, known as the T-26 mod. 1931 and produced by the Bolshevik Plant in Leningrad, were initially assigned to units of the Leningrad Military District. (RGAKFD)

In the event, production was assigned to the Bolshevik Plant in Leningrad, which already had experience in tank manufacturing. Design work to enable mass production of the T-26, as well as subsequent modernization efforts, was led by Semyon A. Ginzburg.

In August 1931, the Soviet authorities adopted a programme for wartime tank production, which called for factories to produce 13,800 T-26s in the first year of a war. This target was clearly unrealistic, as was the actual 1931 production plan, which set a goal of just 500 tanks to be produced at the Bolshevik Plant. By February 1931, this plan was reduced to 300 tanks, with the first to be completed by 1 May. Even this reduced number proved unachievable, however. In the spring of 1931, preparations for serial production of the T-26 were still under way. Meanwhile, two prototype T-26s were being assembled, and the preliminary blueprints were mostly finished by 1 May. The technological process was approved on 16 June, after which the Bolshevik Plant began producing the necessary tools for serial production. The main issue at this point was converting the imperial measurements of the Vickers design to metric measurements.

The first ten T-26s, known as the 'installation batch', were completed in the summer of 1931. A major difference was that the Soviet T-26 mod. 1931 had higher turrets (with an observation slit) than the Vickers 6-Ton tank. Soviet turrets had a rectangular firing port for the Degtyaryov light machine gun, as opposed to the round ports used by the original British design for the Vickers .303in machine gun. The front part of the hull was also slightly modified. Serial production of the T-26 began in August 1931. By the end of the year, 120 had been built – well short of the planned 500 – but the Red Army accepted only 100 due to significant manufacturing defects.

Soviet industry faced great difficulties in adapting to large-scale production of a modern tank design. The Izhorsk Plant in Leningrad struggled to produce armour plate of the prescribed 13mm thickness, and even the 10mm plate produced had too many fractures and imperfections. The engines were noisy and prone to stalling, road wheels shed rubber, transmission gears stripped under load and suspension springs cracked.

In February 1932, the tank-production facilities at the Bolshevik Plant were reorganized into a new factory, Plant No. 174, with Konstantin K. Sirken appointed as director and Ginzburg serving as the chief engineer, overseeing the design bureau known as the *Opytniy Konstruktotorsko-Mekhanicheskiy Otdel* (OKMO: Experimental Design and Mechanical Department). Despite these reorganization efforts, the 1932 production plan could not be fulfilled. In April, Sirken reported that delays in T-26 assembly were primarily due to subcontractors' slow deliveries of components and assemblies, many of which were of poor quality. The rejection rates for engines were as high as 88 per cent; for armoured hulls, 41 per cent. In 1932, Plant No. 174 produced 1,410 T-26s and submitted 1,361 for acceptance, but the Red Army accepted only 950.

In 1932, the Soviet Union launched its 'Great Tank Programme', which included a short-term goal of producing 3,000 T-26s. Throughout the 1932 production run, the OKMO made various modifications to the T-26 design. The Izhorsk Plant began transitioning from riveted to welded construction. Owing to a lack of tools and trained personnel, however, some T-26s had welded hulls and turrets, some were riveted and others featured a mix of both construction methods.

By early 1932, discussions began regarding enhancement of the T-26's armament. The machine-gun-armed version of the tank was found to be insufficient for destroying enemy fortifications and defending against other tanks, so in March 1932 a T-26 was fitted with a small turret from the experimental T-35-1 heavy tank, armed with a 37mm PS-2 main gun. In April, two additional T-26s were tested with these turrets. The PS-2 had excellent characteristics for its time, but it was ultimately not adopted by the Red Army, which preferred the German 3.7cm KwK 37 gun. A Soviet version of this gun, the B-3 (5K), was then developed. The B-3 had a smaller recoil and breech block, which allowed it to be mounted in the standard T-26 machine-gun turret with minimal modifications. The Kalinin Plant in Leningrad, however, responsible for manufacturing the B-3, struggled to produce enough of them. The guns produced from the summer of 1932 onwards were allocated to the BT-2 light tank programme instead of the T-26 programme. Consequently, the T-26's right-side machine-gun turret was armed with the 37mm PS-1 (or 'Hotchkiss-PS') gun. Roughly 450 of the 1,627 twin-turret T-26s produced between 1931 and 1933 were equipped with the PS-1 gun.

A Red Army tank battalion during field exercises in the early 1930s, equipped with T-26 mod. 1932 (foreground) and mod. 1931 (background) tanks, armed with a 37mm PS-2 cannon in the right turret and a machine gun in the left turret. The riveted turret construction and the arrangement of the observation slits are clearly visible. (CMVS)

A close-up view of a T-26 mod. 1933, featuring a single turret and a 45mm 20K main gun capable of engaging tanks, machine-gun nests and various strongholds. Effective fire could only be provided from a stationary position, which exposed the T-26 to enemy anti-tank gun fire. (Author's Collection)

In March 1932, the Red Army adopted the new 45mm 19K anti-tank gun, developed at Plant No. 8. Soon after, a tank-mounted version, the 20K, which was improved with a semi-automatic breech instead of the original 'quarter-automatic' version, became available. (A 'quarter-automatic' gun's sliding breech block closed automatically once a shell was loaded, but unlike semi-automatic guns, the fired shell casing had to be manually ejected by opening the breech block.) Other changes were in the elevation mechanism and the recoil system. In December 1932, the Soviet authorities ordered that T-26s be fitted with the 20K gun and a DT light machine gun. A new, larger single turret was also designed to accommodate the gun, with production starting in the spring of 1933. Delays in gun manufacturing meant that no T-26 with the new gun was completed until June, however. The production of periscopic sights was delayed as well, not becoming available until late 1933, further postponing Red Army acceptance of the new tank model.

Production of the single-turret T-26 was hampered by lingering reliability issues with the new 20K mod. 1932 gun. The improved version of the gun, sometimes designated the 45mm mod. 1932/34, entered production in December 1933 and largely resolved the issues. The version of the T-26 with the 20K gun is often referred to as the T-26 mod. 1933, but this designation was in fact coined by tank historians. At the time, however, the two main T-26 versions were referred to as *dvukhbashennyi* ('twin-turret') and *odnobashennyi* ('single-turret') models.

In 1933, the UMM approved the installation of the new 71-TK-1 tank radio in the T-26. While experimental installations of this radio had been tested in twin-turret T-26s, it became standard only in single-turret T-26s, which came to be known as *radiyniy* ('radio') tanks, in contrast to the *lineyniy* ('line') tanks. The 'radio' tanks were easily identifiable by the prominent, frame-style 'horseshoe' antenna mounted around the turret, and were revealed to the world during the October Revolution Day Parade in Moscow's Red Square on 7 November 1933.

By 1936, the T-26 was considered one of the best infantry-support tanks worldwide, but it still faced several technical issues that impacted its performance. The manufacturing quality of the Soviet-made engine was inferior compared to its British original, and the engine's cooling problems persisted. As a result, the T-26's practical maximum road speed was about half of its nominal value. Additionally, due to poor manufacturing quality, the service life of the Soviet engine was short, requiring an overhaul after only 250 hours of use. The engine also struggled with cold-weather starts. To fix the problem, the Soviet designers gave the driver an additional magneto, which could be used to help with starting, but even this solution was somewhat unreliable. The engine could also be started with a winch.

To address the engine issues, the T-26 was upgraded with imported Scintilla and Bosch starters, along with other improvements that boosted horsepower from 93PS to 96PS. Crew protection was enhanced with the addition of an escape hatch in the tank's belly; and a new turret with sloped armour was introduced. The suspension was also upgraded by thickening the springs from 5.5mm to 6mm. The fuel-tank capacity was increased, which increased the T-26's weight to 9.6 tonnes.

In 1937, some T-26s were fitted with turret-mounted DT anti-aircraft light machine guns, spotlights for 'combat lighting' and new VCU-3 and TPU-3 communication devices. Between 1937 and 1939, one in every five T-26s was equipped with two 'combat light' searchlights for night operations. The engine was upgraded to 95PS. That year, only radio-equipped T-26s fitted with 71-TK-3 radios were produced, with an ammunition capacity of 147 main-gun rounds and 3,087 machine-gun cartridges. The T-26's weight increased to 9.75 tonnes.

Despite the rearming of the T-26 with a 45mm main gun, no major efforts were made to improve the tank's armour, which by the mid-1930s was insufficient for battlefield protection. It would not be entirely accurate to say no steps were taken to improve the T-26's armour protection, however, because in 1938 the tank received a conical turret, sloped armour, and an angled front plate, improving its resistance to small-arms fire. The armour still offered no protection against anti-tank shells, however; and radical improvements in armour protection were simply not feasible because increasing the weight of the armour would have overloaded the T-26's chassis, engine and transmission.

In 1937–38, 20K main guns produced for the T-26 received an electric firing mechanism and telescopic sights. Two additional fuel tanks increased the tank's range. Combat weight reached 10.28 tonnes. The configuration of T-26s with conical turrets differed depending on whether they had radios, additional machine guns or searchlights.

As a comprehensive re-armouring of the T-26 would have required a complete redesign, expedient measures were taken. The hull sides of newly produced tanks were reinforced to 20mm by adding an appliqué extension on the upper hull superstructure. This feature appeared first on the final production batches of tanks fitted with the T-26 mod. 1938 turret, which was subsequently modified again with the introduction of a new stamped mantlet in place of the original welded mantlet.

In 1938, the T-26 was equipped with a conical turret featuring the 45mm mod. 1934 gun. Main guns produced in 1937 and 1938 were fitted with an electric firing mechanism and TOP-1 (later TOS) stabilization telescopic sights.

In 1939, the T-26 was again modernized, introducing sloped armour at the turret base, additional ammunition storage and an upgraded communication system. In January 1939, the rear turret ball machine-gun mount was removed. The engine's compression was increased, raising the output to 97PS, and changes were made to the suspension. These updates distinguished this 1939 version from earlier T-26 models.

T-26 tank production 1931–41*												
	1931	1932	1933	1934	1935	1936	1937	1938	1939	1940	1941	**TOTAL**
Factory No. 174 (Voroshilov)												
T-26 (twin turret)	100	1,361	576	1	–	–	–	–	–	–	–	2,038
T-26 (single turret)	–	–	693	489	553	447	–	–	945	1,018	47**	4,192
T-26 (single turret with radio)	–	–	20	457	650	826	550	716	350	318	–	3,887
Stalingrad Tractor Factory												
T-26	–	–	5	23	115	?	–	30	?	10	–	183(?)
TOTAL	100	1,361	1,294	970	1,318	1,273(?)	550	746	1,295(?)	1,346	47	10,300(?)

* Excluding all specialized versions, e.g. self-propelled artillery mountings.   ** Other sources give a total of 116.

The T-26's vulnerable engine radiator cover was replaced in the summer of 1939 with a new cover that became known as the 'rumble seat' by tank crews. Internal ammunition stowage was increased to 186 rounds of 45mm ammunition (165 in radio-equipped tanks). The improved PTK commander's vision device, which had previously been used only in radio-equipped tanks, was now issued to all T-26s. The 71-TK-1 radio was replaced with the more modern 71-TK-3, and the rail antenna was replaced with a whip antenna in January 1939. The suspension was upgraded again, with the spring bundle being increased from three to five leaves. This upgrade package was known as the T-26-1 or T-26 mod. 1939. Some of these tanks were equipped with an anti-aircraft machine-gun mount on the turret roof.

The final updates to the T-26 came in 1940 during the Winter War (1939–40) against Finland. Some tanks were equipped with armour screens, and the cemented armour of the turret base was replaced with homogeneous armour. Other refinements included a unified viewing device, improvements to the turret ring and better fuel tanks. The T-26's weight, with the addition of armour screens, now exceeded 12 tonnes, which negatively impacted its technical reliability.

A T-26 mod. 1937 in Finland, December 1939. (Finnish Wartime Photograph Archive/ Wikimedia/CC BY-SA 4.0)

T-26 mod. 1936

Soviet tanks produced from 1935–36 onwards were painted with ZB AU (alkyd-urethane protective base) green paint, which was used until 1939 as it was discovered that this pigment mixture reflected light differently from chlorophyll, giving it a noticeably different appearance from surrounding vegetation. As a result, the Red Army discontinued the use of ZB AU and adopted 4BO as the new standard camouflage paint in 1939. The Soviet Armoured Vehicles Department recommended using existing ZB AU stocks as a primer rather than discarding them, however. Most T-26s supplied to Spain retained ZB AU paint, often supplemented by a one- or two-digit tactical number, sometimes preceded by the letter 'C' for 'Carro' ('tank'), along with various slogans (e.g. 'Long live Madrid', 'Long live Central Army').

Crew	3
Length	4.62m
Width	2.44m
Height	2.19m
Combat weight	9.6 tonnes
Main gun	45mm 20Kmod. 1934, 102 rounds
Elevation	n/a
Machine guns	two 7.62mm DT
Radio	71-TK-1
Engine	GAZ T-26
Fuel capacity	290 litres
Range (on roads)	220–40km
Top speed	31.1km/h
Armour	15mm gun mantlet, 15mm full front, sides and turret

The first encounters between the PzKpfw I and the T-26 mod. 1938/39 were notably amicable, as both types found themselves on the same side during the German invasion of Poland in 1939. The T-26 mod. 1938 could be recognized by the twin combat lights mounted above the main gun, and its conical turret. This photograph was taken during the joint Soviet–German victory parade in Brest-Litovsk on 22 September 1939, a symbolic event marking the successful partitioning of Poland. (Author's Collection)

Total production of 'single- and 'twin-turret' T-26s during 1931–41 exceeded 10,000, of which 281 were sent to Spain. By the start of Operation *Barbarossa*, the Axis invasion of the Soviet Union on 22 June 1941, the Red Army in the western military districts still had 4,875 T-26, approximately 85 per cent of which were new or operational, while the remaining examples required repairs or major overhauls.

T-26 and PzKpfw I models compared

Tank model	T-26 mod. 1935 (radio tank)	T-26 mod. 1936	PzKpfw I Ausf A	PzKpfw I Ausf B
Crew	3	3	2	2
Dimensions (L × W × H)	4.62m × 2.44m × 2.24m	4.62m × 2.44m × 2.19m	4.02m × 2.06m × 1.72m	4.42m × 2.06m × 1.72m
Loaded weight	9.6 tonnes	9.65 tonnes	5.4 tonnes	5.8 tonnes
Main gun	45mm (20K)	45mm (20K)	–	–
Armour penetration @ 100m @ 0 degrees	~52mm	~52mm	–	–
Machine gun	1/2 × 7.62mm (DT)	1 × 7.62mm (DT)	2 × 7.92mm (MG 13)	2 × 7.92mm (MG 13)
Armour penetration @ 100m @ 0 degrees	–	–	~15mm	~15mm
Main-gun range	3,600m	3,600m	800m	800m
Armour (front/bottom)	15mm to 6mm	15mm to 6mm	13mm to 6mm	13mm to 6mm
Engine	90PS (GAZ four-cylinder)	90PS (GAZ four-cylinder)	60PS (Krupp M305)	100PS (Maybach NL38 Tr)
Radio communications	71-TK-1 (frame antenna)	–	Fu 2 (receiver)	Fu 2 (receiver)
Maximum road speed	31.1km/h	31.1km/h	37.5km/h	40km/h
Cross-country speed	22km/h	22km/h	10–12km/h	12–15km/h
Cross-country range	130–140km	130–140km	93km	115km
Ground pressure	0.66kg/cm^2	0.66kg/cm^2	n/a	0.52kg/cm^2

PzKpfw I

The Versailles Treaty sought to limit Germany's war-making capabilities by restricting the country's military to a force of just 100,000 men (the Reichswehr) and prohibiting the production or possession of various modern weapon systems, including tanks and armoured cars. Paragraph 24 of the treaty stipulated a fine of 100,000 Marks and imprisonment of up to six months for anyone involved in the manufacture of armoured vehicles, tanks or similar machines with potential military use.

To bypass these restrictions, the German–Soviet Treaty of Rapallo was signed on 16 April 1922. This agreement saw both former adversaries renounce all territorial and financial claims against one another. Secret clauses of the treaty led to the establishment of several German testing and training facilities in the Soviet Union, including the Panzertruppenschule Kama armoured-vehicle testing base. Between 1926 and 1933, companies like Friedrich Krupp AG, Rheinmetall-Borsig AG and Daimler-Benz AG used the base to test new tank prototypes, including the *Leichttraktor* (light tractor) and *Grosstraktor* (heavy multi-turret tractor) designs. Neither of these met the expected specifications, however, prompting a new light-tank prototype design within Germany itself at the beginning of 1930.

In February 1930, representatives from Krupp met with the development committee of Waffenprüfamt 6 (the Weapons Office for Armoured Vehicles and Motorized Equipment under the Army Ordnance Department) to discuss the *Kleintraktor* (small armoured tractor) project. The goal was to create a simple and cost-effective machine that could serve as a military scouting vehicle, weapons carrier and light towing vehicle. Although Waffenprüfamt 6 was initially sceptical that a chassis of this size could be suitable for a light tank, Krupp was tasked with designing a small armoured fighting vehicle armed with a 2cm machine gun, powered by a 60PS air-cooled engine, with a total weight not exceeding 3 tonnes. Krupp was also asked to provide a proposed chassis design, a wooden model for various superstructures and a suspension system for trials at the Kummersdorf testing facility, located 40km south of Berlin.

The prototype of the Krupp *Leichttraktor* (light tractor) was showcased at Wünsdorf in 1934 and served as the predecessor to the *Kleintraktor* (small armoured tractor). (Author's Collection)

Owing to poor experiences during testing of the *Leichttraktor*, which had a tendency to throw tracks (blamed on the rear drive and track tensioner with springs), Waffenprüfamt 6 requested that Krupp redesign the *Kleintraktor* with a front drive and rear-mounted engine, similar to British Carden-Loyd light tractors. To assist Krupp, Waffenprüfamt 6 arranged the purchase of three Carden-Loyd tractors from Vickers via a front company, Aug. Nowack AG Verkaufszentrale. These tractors arrived at Kummersdorf in January 1932, but some sources suggest that two Carden-Loyd chassis, previously purchased by the Soviet Union in 1929, were handed over to the Germans for payment, and used as a design benchmark by German engineers.

The redesigned *Kleintraktor* chassis was first demonstrated to Waffenprüfamt 6 on 29 July 1932, when it was driven around the factory yard on a rough stone surface. The vehicle proved to be highly manoeuvrable, even with the idler wheel lowered. Further trials were conducted at Essen to identify any deficiencies that could be corrected, and then the vehicle was sent to Meppen, where it was demonstrated to a larger contingent from Waffenprüfamt 6 on 15–16 August 1932. Observations from these trials noted the vehicle's soft suspension, which absorbed shocks from small obstacles without causing sway, and its excellent steering ability, allowing it to turn on the spot and steer through shallow curves on the road. Gear shifting was smooth, and there was no tendency for the track to climb up. After installing a stronger spring in the forward road-wheel mount, the chassis stood level. Top speed was only 28km/h, however, attributed to the weak engine (less than 52PS) and insufficient clearance between the road wheels and tracks. The chassis weight of about 2,950kg exceeded the specification by 300kg.

The first *Kleintraktor* was officially accepted by Waffenprüfamt 6 on 19 September 1932 and sent by rail to Kummersdorf, arriving on 26 September. Comparison trials with the Carden-Loyd tractor were held in Wünsdorf on 28 September, where it was demonstrated that the *Kleintraktor* outperformed the Carden-Loyd chassis at speeds of up to 40km/h.

On 1 July 1933, Krupp was officially informed that the firm would receive a contract to produce 150 *Kleintraktoren*, codenamed *Landwirtschaftliche Schlepper* (agricultural

A turretless 1. Serie/LaS, also known as the 'Krupp Tractor', with protective rails around the crew compartment, being used for tank-driver training in spring 1934. Altogether, 150 were produced before the appearance of the PzKpfw I Ausf A, and used by replacement training units until 1940–41. (Author's Collection)

tractor), abbreviated to LaS. These 150 chassis, produced in 1934 without turrets or superstructures, were delivered to the Kraftfahrlehrkommando Zossen and Ohrdruf for tank-driver training. To maintain the secrecy of Germany's covert training of military personnel to operate armoured vehicles, the chassis were disguised with the label 'Krupp-Traktor' in the driver's training manual. Additionally, they were painted field grey, the colour used for commercial vehicles acquired by the Reichswehr, rather than the three-colour camouflage pattern typically applied to combat vehicles.

In June 1933, Waffenprüfamt 6 informed Krupp that the Reichswehrministerium (Ministry of Defence) planned to place large orders for *Kleintraktoren* fitted with armour and equipped with weapons-carrying superstructures. In addition to Krupp, several other large industrial firms – Rheinmetall (assembled at Borsig-Werken in Berlin), MAN, Gutehoffnungshütte and Henschel – were to be involved in production. Contracts were expected to be awarded by 1 October 1933, with deliveries beginning on 1 February 1934. Production goals were set to about 25 units per month.

On 12 October 1932, Generalmajor Oswald Lutz, Inspector of Motor Transport Troops, expressed satisfaction with the *Kleintraktor*'s performance during the Kummersdorf demonstration and requested that Krupp estimate how long it would take to produce five *Kleintraktoren mit M.G.-Turm* ('turrets carrying two machine guns'). The initial plan for a 2cm gun was delayed, as the mounting process for such a weapon was now expected to take up to two years. The decision to delay was intended to facilitate quicker production and the rapid deployment of tanks, but it compromised the combat effectiveness of the vehicles. The *Kleintraktor* was primarily seen as a training tank at this stage.

The ground rules for the turret design specified that it needed to be bulletproof against armour-piercing rounds, and that previous weight restrictions for tanks could be exceeded. Initially, no optical gun sight was proposed; the gunner would aim the shoulder-mounted gun through slits in Kinon glass, using a normal blade sight. This was later modified when a *Zielfernrohr* (telescopic sight) was added to the turret.

While Krupp had a natural advantage in developing the turret due to its longstanding experience in gun production, Daimler-Benz (Berlin-Marienfelde) was asked to provide a competitive design in March 1933. The first of five *Kleintraktoren* equipped with machine-gun turrets, each housing a single 7.92mm MG 13 Dreyse light machine gun, was completed in July 1933, followed by the remaining four in August 1933. As the need for a turret and superstructure design became more urgent, the Reichswehrministerium (Defence Ministry) decided in July 1934 to produce 1,000 LaS tanks with turrets, to be ready for troops by 1 July 1935.

A 1. Serie/LaS participating in training exercises in 1934, during which the crew demonstrated the vehicle's versatility by navigating rough terrain. The open compartment, lacking a turret, provided the driver with a full 360-degree view, thus offering a better understanding of the tank's mobility. (Author's Collection)

Development of the unarmoured vehicles continued, and by the time the first hulls made from special 8mm-thick steel were delivered to Krupp in Essen, they had already been tested against 7.92mm SmK (*Spitzgeschoss mit Kern*: 'pointed bullet with [hardened] core') armour-piercing machine-gun rounds fired from 30m range, which penetrated the hull. In response, Waffenprüfamt 6 requested that the thickness of the frontal sloped wall be increased to 13mm, which would result in a weight increase and put additional strain on the front road wheels, but this was deemed acceptable due to the importance of greater armour protection.

By mid-January 1934, production of the first 200 *M.G. Kampfwagen* ('machine-gun-equipped tanks') or 2. Serie/LaS vehicles had been agreed upon for the 1934 acquisition programme. The order was placed with Daimler-Benz, Krupp-Grusonwerk, Henschel, MAN and Rheinmetall, which were tasked with producing 30 light tanks each, while Krupp-Essen would produce 50.

Initially, the 2. Serie/LaS vehicles did not include radios, but work on modifications to rectify this began in the spring of 1934. The engines were outfitted with more powerful electrical generators to support a Fu 2 radio receiver in the hull, its signal being transferred electromagnetically to the turret and the commander, who used headphones but no microphones. Radio transmitters and receivers were only installed on the *kleiner Panzerbefehlswagen* (smaller command tanks).

On 25 April 1934, the delivery schedule for the 200 LaS engines was set at 50 per month from October 1934 to January 1935. This production rate was considered adequate to meet the chassis delivery schedule, which was expected to be completed by the end of February 1935. By early June, however, just a month before the official decision was made to increase the LaS order to 1,000 vehicles, Krupp was asked to produce 550 engines for a third LaS series by 31 May 1935. The additional 550 tanks (initially identified as 3. Serie) were contracted as follows: 215 chassis from Krupp, 60 from Rheinmetall, 65 from Daimler-Benz, 100 from Henschel and 110 from MAN. In December 1935, the last 175 chassis, powered by Krupp air-cooled engines, were ordered as the 4. Serie/LaS.

By August 1935, the official nomenclature was changed, and the LaS vehicle was now designated as the Panzerkampfwagen (PzKpfw) I. By April 1936, it was officially known as the PzKpfw I Ausf A (or SdKfz 101). Total production of the PzKpfw I Ausf A, built in three series (2. to 4. Serie/LaS) from October 1934 to October 1936, was 1,160 vehicles.

Operational use of the PzKpfw I Ausf A revealed several shortcomings, the most notable being the insufficient power of the Krupp M305 petrol engine. Attempts to replace the M305 with the Krupp M601 diesel engine proved unsatisfactory. As a result, the M305 was replaced by the Maybach NL38 TR petrol engine; but installing this larger engine necessitated rebuilding the hull, extending the engine compartment by 400mm and modifying the top and rear shields to accommodate the damper. The modifications in turn required a change to the chassis, including the addition of an extra pair of road wheels and a return roller.

The extended version of the PzKpfw I, designated the PzKpfw I Ausf B, was initially produced at the Henschel and Krupp (Magdeburg) plants, and from 1936, at the MAN plant in Nuremberg and the Wegmann plant in Kassel. Overhauls for both

A *Befehlswagen* (command tank) fabricated on the hull of the *Krupp Leichttraktor* alongside the first batch of 1. Serie/LaS tanks with superstructures and turrets fabricated from mild steel. (Author's Collection)

variants were carried out at the original manufacturing plants, as well as at the newly seized Českomoravská-Kolben-Daněk plant in Prague (renamed Böhmische-Mährische Machinenfabrik (BMM) after the annexation of Bohemia and Moravia), and at Škoda in Pilsen.

From October 1934 to October 1936, total production of the PzKpfw I Ausf A, from the 2. to 4. Serie/LaS, reached 1,160 vehicles. Production of the PzKpfw I Ausf B totalled 403 vehicles, produced between August 1936 and August 1937. Germany supplied 122 to Spain: 96 PzKpfw I Ausf A, 21 PzKpfw I Ausf B, four Befehlswagen I command tanks and one turretless (LaS) training tank.

The great majority of PzKpfw Is, numbering nearly 1,500 vehicles, stayed in Germany and formed the backbone of the German *Panzerwaffe* (Armoured Force) at the outset of World War II. These tanks were deployed from September 1939 to June 1941 during campaigns in Poland, Scandinavia, France, the Low Countries and the Balkans. By the time of the German invasion of the Soviet Union in June 1941, the PzKpfw I fleet was already obsolete. Owing to limitations in the availability of modern tanks, however, the German Army assigned 152 PzKpfw Is to front-line Panzer divisions in the East. Additionally, approximately 150 PzKpfw Is, many of which had been converted into the *Ladungsleger* (explosive-charge carrier) variant, served as support vehicles with the *Panzerpionierkompanie* (armoured pioneer/combat-engineer companies) of the Panzer divisions in the East.

This photograph of a PzKpfw I Ausf A, showcasing a clear view of its suspension, features four road wheels supported by a distinctive horizontal girder, along with a larger idler wheel. (Author's Collection)

PzKpfw I Ausf B

German armoured fighting vehicles introduced in the early 1930s were painted with a *Buntfarbenanstrich* ('multi-coloured paint pattern') consisting of green (*Grün*, RAL 6007), sand (*Erdgelb*, RAL 8002) and brown (*Braun*, RAL 8010). While operating in Spain, PzKpfw Is were marked with tricolour national flags and tactical symbols. Three-digit numbers (e.g. '450') were used, with the first digit indicating the company. Geometric shapes represented the battalions – a diamond for the 1st Tank Battalion, a circle for the 2nd Tank Battalion – and the letter 'M' indicated the commander's vehicle. The emblem of the Spanish Legion, featuring crossed muskets, a crossbow and a halberd, served as the formation identifier. The upper part of the tank turret was painted white with a black St Andrew's saltire, used for air recognition.

Crew	2
Length	4.42m
Width	2.06m
Height	1.72m
Combat weight	5.8 tonnes
Main gun	n/a
Machine guns	two 7.92mm MG 13
Elevation	−10 to +20 degrees
Radio	Fu 2 (receiver only)
Engine	Maybach NL 38TR
Fuel capacity	146 litres
Range (on roads)	170km
Top speed	40km/h
Armour	15mm gun mantlet, 13mm full front, sides and turret

TECHNICAL SPECIFICATIONS

LAYOUT AND COMMUNICATIONS

The T-26 was divided into three compartments: the driving-transmission compartment, the fighting compartment (including the turret) and the engine compartment. The hull was box-shaped in cross-section, and the cylindrical turret, mounted on a ball-bearing race, could traverse 360 degrees. The turret was offset to the left of the centreline and closed at the top with its roof, featuring a one-piece hatch for the commander/gunner and a one-piece hatch for the loader or loader/radio operator.

In the twin-turret T-26, the driver sat low in the front left of the hull, while each of the small turrets was manned by a single crewman who doubled as gunner, loader and commander for his weapon – a cramped and inefficient arrangement compared to the later single-turret design. The single-turret T-26 had a crew of three: a driver/mechanic in the front of the hull; a loader on the right side of the turret; and the commander/gunner on the left side of the turret, who also served as the radio operator. The driver controlled the vehicle using a steering wheel and track steering levers on either side of his seat, which activated the double-radius steering gears and a power-assisted steering wheel. The driver had a vision port located in the front armour of the hull and a set of engine controls, a compass and a clock, all located on a console to the left of the seat.

A column of T-26s led by radio-equipped examples, which were to be deployed in large numbers to provide effective communication during rapid advances of tank formations supporting infantry forces. None of the Soviet Union's potential enemies in the mid-1930s possessed such communication capabilities. (RGAKFD)

For situational awareness, the commander relied on a panoramic periscope. The 45mm 20K main gun was equipped with a telescopic TOP mod. 1930 sight, offering 2.5× magnification and a 15-degree field of view for both the gun and machine gun. Additionally, a PT-1 periscope gun sight, ranged up to 3,600m, was mounted on the turret roof. This sight was mechanically linked to the gun mount and could serve as an alternative means of aiming the 45mm gun. Like the telescope, it had 2.5× magnification, but offered a wider field of view (26 degrees). The sight could be traversed through a half-circle, making it the commander's principal external observation device. A second periscopic sight could be mounted on the right side of the turret for use by the loader, though due to the cost of these sights, most tanks only had one. Some later-production T-26s were equipped with a TOS sight, which was gyro-stabilized along the vertical axis.

Early on, communication between the commander and driver was facilitated by a 'speaking tube', later replaced by a light-signalling system. From 1933, T-26s were fitted with a 71-TK-1 short-wave radio set, which worked with a rail antenna mounted around the turret. The fragile radio equipment often failed, however, due to vibrations. During the Spanish Civil War (1936–39), radio-equipped tanks experienced complete disruption of their radios after initial battles, with antennas often dismounted. This was partly due to enemy anti-tank guns targeting the easily recognizable radio tanks. In Spain, communication within platoons and companies was primarily conducted using coloured flags. This method was ineffective and dangerous, as flags could easily be misidentified in poor light, and the visible use of flags by the platoon commander made him a target for enemy fire. As a result, the use of flags was largely abandoned by the group commanded by Captain Pavel Arman (real name Pauls Tiltiņš) in the autumn of 1936 and was not widely used thereafter.

The PzKpfw I was divided into three compartments: the driving-transmission compartment, the fighting compartment (including the turret) and the engine compartment. The turret, which could be traversed 360 degrees by hand, was mounted on a ball-bearing race to the right of the vehicle's centreline. The turret was sealed at the top by a one-piece hatch. Entry and exit for the commander was through the small turret roof, while the driver entered and exited the vehicle via a hinged rectangular door located on the left side of the superstructure.

The T-26's 45mm main gun could fire both the UO-243 high-explosive round (left) and the BR-243 armour-piercing round (right).

27

T-26 TURRET

1. 45mm ammunition stowage
2. Left-side vision port
3. Turret-rotation wheel
4. Gunner's telescopic sight
5. 45mm 20K main gun
6. Gun-elevation handwheel
7. Coaxial DT light machine gun
8. Periscope sight
9. Loader's seat
10. Rear DT light machine gun

PzKpfw I TURRET

1. Commander/gunner's seat
2. Turret fastener
3. Magazine for 25 rounds
4. Spare magazine box
5. Light machine guns (MG 13)
6. Gunner's te escopic sight
7. Turret rotat on wheel
8. Right rear vision port
9. Headrest pad

Despite being equipped with radio receivers, PzKpfw I crews were trained to communicate within their platoon using coloured flags. This method proved to be highly ineffective during the Spanish Civil War, but such flag-based communication continued to be practised on German training grounds until 1940. In this 1937 photograph, a tank commander holds red and yellow flags signifying 'position reached'. (Author's Collection)

The PzKpfw I had a crew of two: a driver and a commander/gunner. The driver sat on the left in the forward hull of the cramped vehicle, while the commander occupied the turret, mounted to the right of the vehicle's centreline. The driver was provided with a set of engine controls, including an oil temperature gauge, a revolution counter marked 0–3,000rpm with a danger zone above 2,500rpm, and a speedometer marked 0–50km/h. The driver operated the vehicle using a wheel and track steering levers on either side of his seat, which activated the double-radius steering gears and a power-assisted steering wheel. The commander's seat was suspended from the turret and rotated with it, although the floor of the fighting compartment remained static.

The Zielfernrohr 1 with 2.5x magnification and a 28-degree field of view (498m wide at 900m range) was used for direct aiming of the armament. The front of the articulated telescope was mounted in the gun mantlet, while the rear was held by a pivoting triangular carrier bolted to the turret roof. The advantage of this design was that the sight was rigidly connected to the armament, eliminating errors between the sight line and the main gun's axis. The small aperture in the gun mantlet, only about 12mm in diameter, made the telescope nearly invulnerable. Together with the inner gun mount, the telescope's head could be elevated through an arc of +20 to -10 degrees. Both crew members also used vision ports with vision slits for close combat observation. Eye protection against lead splash and fragments was provided by a 12mm-thick *Luglas-Glaskombination* (laminated glass block) mounted behind the vision slit.

Communication between the commander and the driver was facilitated by a voice tube. The PzKpfw I was equipped with a FuG 2 radio receiver, which could be used to communicate with an SdKfz 265 Panzerbefehlswagen. This vehicle had the same chassis as the PzKpfw I Ausf B but featured a larger superstructure and was assigned to every tank company. Its crew consisted of three men, as it was equipped with both a radio transmitter (FuG 6) and a receiver (FuG 2), requiring an additional crew member. The FuG 2 worked with a 2m collapsible aerial mounted on the offside of

The 7.92mm Mauser round (left) and the SmKH round (right) used by the PzKpfw I's machine guns.

the hull, operated by a handle inside the fighting compartment. When the turret was traversed, the turret ring automatically lowered the aerial to prevent it from fouling the guns. The prescribed method of communication within the platoon and company also included the use of coloured flags and/or flares.

ARMOUR

The T-26 was protected by 15mm-thick armour plates, except for the hull and turret roof, which were covered by 10mm plates, and the hull bottom, which was protected by 6mm plates. Initially, the armoured plates were fastened to a steel frame using rivets, but when the Izhorsk Plant mastered electric welding technology, a mixed hull construction – combining welded and riveted techniques – was introduced.

The PzKpfw I's armour hull was made from several cemented (hardened) rolled steel plates welded together at the following angles: a 13mm-thick front plate at 25 degrees, an 8mm glacis plate at 70 degrees, 13mm side plates at 0 degrees, a 13mm rear wall at 15 degrees and a 5mm belly plate at 90 degrees. The hull was reinforced by a firewall separating the crew and engine compartments and by three tubular axles secured to the belly and sidewalls. Strong steel strips were bolted along the upper edge of the PzKpfw I's hull for added strength and to secure the superstructure.

The T-26 mod. 1938/39 featured a new sloped-armour turret and sloped side hull armour. This model arrived too late to be shipped to Spain but was used during the Soviet invasion of Poland, the Winter War against Finland and the early stages of the war against Germany. (Author's Collection)

This PzKpfw I Ausf A was knocked out in the Casa de Campo, a hilly and heavily wooded park on the western outskirts of Madrid, in November 1936. (BDH/BNE/CC BY 4.0)

FIREPOWER

The single-turret T-26 was equipped with the 45mm 20K main gun, which was based on Rheinmetall's 3.7cm PaK anti-tank gun. The semi-automatic mechanism worked fully with armour-piercing shells, but for fragmentation shells, it operated like a quarter-automatic system. In this case, the opening of the breech and extraction of the shell casings were performed manually, and the breech would close automatically when a new round was inserted. This was due to the differing initial velocities of armour-piercing and high-explosive shells.

The 45mm ammunition load for radio-equipped T-26s was 82 rounds, while T-26s without radios could carry 122 rounds. The length of the barrel was 2,070mm

A close view of the 20K main gun mounted on a T-26 fielded by the Spanish Legion's 2nd Tank Battalion. (Author's Collection)

A Nationalist PzKpfw I Ausf A on the outskirts of Madrid in early November 1936. (BDH/BNE/CC BY 4.0)

(46 calibres). The armour-piercing shell, weighing 1.425kg, left the barrel with an initial velocity of 760m/sec, which made it capable of penetrating a 43mm-thick armour plate at a distance of 500m. The gun had an elevation range of -6 degrees to +22 degrees, with traverse and elevation controlled by two manipulators.

The secondary weapon was the 7.62mm Degtyaryov DT light machine gun, mounted coaxially next to the main gun. Some tanks were also equipped with a ball mounting at the rear of the turret bustle, allowing for the installation of an additional DT for defence against close infantry attacks. Tanks without radios could carry up to 3,339 rounds of 7.62mm ammunition, while radio-equipped tanks carried only 2,016 rounds.

The PzKpfw I's basic armament consisted of two 7.92mm Dreyse MG 13 light machine guns, each with a rate of fire of 650rd/min and a total of 1,525 rounds in

61 ammunition boxes. Later versions of the PzKpfw I Ausf B, produced from 1936, carried 2,100 rounds in 90 ammunition boxes. Eight ammunition containers were located in the rear of the turret and on the floor of the fighting compartment.

The two MG 13s had all-round traverse and were mounted in tandem but capable of independent fire. The MG 13 on the left was fired using a trigger on the elevating handwheel to the commander's left, while the MG 13 on the right was fired from a trigger on the traverse handwheel to the right. Maximum elevation was +18 degrees; maximum depression was -12 degrees.

MOBILITY

The T-26 was powered by a four-cylinder, air-cooled petrol engine, the GAZ, producing 90PS. This engine was a copy of the British Armstrong Siddeley Puma petrol engine, and enabled the T-26 to reach a nominal speed of up to 31km/h – quite good for its time. The engine was placed longitudinally in the engine compartment, with the flywheel facing forward. A centrifugal fan, mounted in a special casing beneath the engine, circulated cooling air. The engine could be started either with an electric starter ('Scintilla,' 2PS) or by means of a hand-crank starter. The cylinder diameter was 120mm, with a stroke of 146.5mm, and the engine's displacement was 6,600cc. The pistons and engine were made of cast iron, and the compression ratio was 1:4.8. The T-26's power output was 91PS at 2,100rpm, 82PS at 2,000rpm and an economical 75PS at 2,000rpm.

A post-Spanish Civil War photograph of a T-26 in Spanish Army service during field manoeuvres, demonstrating its ability to cross various types of obstacles. (BDH/CC BY 4.0)

The T-26 used leaded light petrol, either from refinery No. 1 in Grozny or aviation petrol No. 91. The fuel supply was managed by a Type ML mechanical fuel pump and an emergency manual pump. On the right side of the engine, there was an oil tank. The two-speed oil pump was driven by the engine, and to lubricate a dry engine, 25kg of Type MD mineral oil was required.

The mechanical transmission system included a single-plate dry friction clutch, a Cardan shaft, a five-speed gearbox, steering clutches, final drives and band brakes mounted on the final drive housings. The gearbox was located to the left of the driver, and the driveshaft connected the transmission and the engine, passing through the combat compartment. The transmission allowed the T-26 to turn with a minimum radius equal to the 2.18m width of the tank's track. The running gear consisted of a guide wheel, a drive wheel, eight double road wheels and four double support rollers.

The gearbox (five forward speeds and one reverse) was operated hydraulically, with the gear lever positioned to the left of the driver's seat. The suspension on each side consisted of eight paired rubberized road wheels (each 300mm in diameter) grouped into four bogies with quarter-elliptic leaf springs, four rubberized return rollers (each 254mm in diameter), an idler wheel with a tensioning crank and a front-mounted drive wheel with detachable toothed rings for sprocket engagement.

The steel track featured single track links, each consisting of a main link with a single guide horn, a connecting link with three end connectors and two linking pins. This design minimized power loss, though the tracks could occasionally climb onto the sprocket, resulting in jams or thrown tracks. Additionally, the sprocket teeth wore unevenly, leading to destructive stresses on the internal drive components.

A convoy of Red Army T-26 mod. 1933 tanks during a break in field manoeuvres in the summer of 1939. Note that the tank's crew members are wearing dark-blue uniforms and sidecaps, instead of the typical soft helmet, the TSh-4, which was designed to provide protection inside the tanks. (Author's Collection)

Track length was 1,700mm, consisting of 108 or 109 links. Track width was 260mm, with a base of 90mm. The weight of each track link was 2.7kg.

The combat weight of T-26s produced in 1933–34 was 9.4 tonnes. After the installation of a radio station and an additional fuel tank in 1935, the weight increased to 9.6 tonnes, and later to 9.65 tonnes.

The PzKpfw I Ausf A was powered by the Krupp M305 engine, a four-cylinder boxer, overhead-valve, air-cooled engine. The cylinder diameter was 90mm, the stroke was 130mm and the engine displacement was 3,460cc. The pistons and engine block were made of cast iron. The compression ratio was 1:5.2, and the engine produced 60PS at 2,500rpm. The aluminium block had two covers: the upper cover supported the fuel pump and magneto with its drive; the lower cover contained the oil pan. The cylinders were arranged flat, with two on the left and two on the right. The engine was equipped with a generator, starter, magneto, two Solex carburettors, pressurized lubrication, an oil filter, oil cooler and a cooling fan.

Power from the engine was transmitted to the gearbox via Cardan shafts. The gearbox was the ZF Aphon FG 35 (Ausf A) or ZF Aphon FG 31 (Ausf B), with five forward gears and one reverse gear in the Ausf B. The maximum recommended speeds in each gear were as follows: 1st, 5km/h; 2nd, 11km/h; 3rd, 20km/h; 4th, 32km/h; and 5th, 42km/h.

From the engine, the drive passed through a two-plate dry clutch to the gearbox, which provided one reverse and five forward gears. The drive then passed across the front of the PzKpfw I to the drive sprockets. Steering was achieved through the use of the clutch and brake, with cooling provided by a small fan. The driver controlled the

The PzKpfw I Ausf A, with its narrow tracks, performed well on firm ground but struggled in extremely muddy conditions. While mobility was the PzKpfw I's strong point, its armament of only two MG 13 light machine guns and thin armour meant it was no match for Soviet tanks. (Author's Collection)

tank's direction with steering levers, each of which was fitted with two handgrips: one for normal steering and the other with a thumb plunger to act as a parking brake (there was no separate handbrake).

The suspension on each side of the vehicle consisted of a drive wheel with an exchangeable sprocket, road wheels, an idler wheel and three return rollers. The track was tensioned around the suspension on both sides. The idler wheels (600mm in diameter) were situated at the rear and equipped with a screw mechanism for adjusting track tension. The first road wheel had a shock absorber, while the remaining three or four road wheels featured bogies with longitudinal quarter-elliptic springs. Sprockets with 21 driving teeth drove the tracks from the front of the vehicle.

Operational use of the PzKpfw I Ausf A revealed that its engine power was insufficient, prompting the installation of the 100PS Maybach NL38 TR six-cylinder petrol engine. The gearbox was also replaced. Fitting the new, larger engine required modifications to the hull, however. The length of the engine compartment was extended by 400mm, and its top and rear shields were rebuilt to accommodate the new engine, with dampers fixed to the rear (in the Ausf A variant, the dampers were mounted on the mudguards). The extension of the hull necessitated further modifications to the chassis, including the addition of an extra pair of road wheels and return rollers, as well as changes to the road-wheel bracket mounting. Aside from these changes, the PzKpfw I Ausf B remained almost identical to its Ausf A predecessor.

A PzKpfw I Ausf B drives over a brick-built obstacle during a *Panzersportsfest* at the Wünsdorf training ground in 1936. Despite its small size, the PzKpfw I was capable of overcoming various terrain obstacles and shallow streams, allowing it to exploit breakthroughs quickly and effectively. (Author's Collection)

37

THE COMBATANTS

After the 1936 elections in Spain resulted in the formation of a Frente Popular (Popular Front) government, supported mainly by left-wing parties, a military uprising began in garrison towns across the country. This uprising was led by Nationalists and supported by conservative elements within the clergy, military, landowners and fascist groups such as the Falange. The *Ejército de la República Española*, Spain's national army, was divided between the opposing factions, with most of the combat-experienced troops joining the Nationalist forces.

Prior to the Spanish Civil War, the operational experience of Spanish tank crews was limited to colonial engagements in northern Morocco. Beginning in March 1922, an armoured company of FT-17s saw its first combat action while operating alongside the newly formed Spanish Legion. The conflict concluded in May 1926, after which the armoured company returned to the Spanish mainland. The main shortcomings of the Moroccan campaign were a lack of coordination between tanks and supporting infantry, and the difficulty of operating in harsh, mountainous terrain. These issues would resurface during the Spanish Civil War, particularly as Spain's geography presented substantial obstacles to the effective employment of mechanized forces. While improvements in tactical coordination could be made through training, the terrain remained an immutable challenge.

The small Spanish armoured force, consisting of fewer than 30 World War I-era French tanks, was also split almost equally between the two sides, both of which urgently needed to increase their number of armoured fighting vehicles. As Spanish industry was unable to produce a significant number of modern tanks, both sides turned to foreign countries for support; Italy and Germany quickly aligned with the Nationalists, while the Soviet Union supported the Republicans. While the delivery of new equipment was critical, equally important was the need to train Spanish tank personnel and develop relevant tactical approaches. This required the assistance of foreign advisors, instructors and technical staff.

REPUBLICANS AND SOVIET PERSONNEL

The Republicans were the first to begin preparing their tank personnel for training by appointing Colonel Rafael Sánchez-Paredes, a skilled organizer, as the head of the Archena Tank Base on 22 September 1936. He was tasked with establishing a tank school before the arrival of Soviet instructors and equipment. Archena was chosen for its location away from the front lines, its proximity to the port of Cartagena (the main base of the Republican Navy), and its connection to the national highway to Madrid, the primary war front. The tank driving and shooting school, along with repair workshops and a mechanical training centre, were set up at the Miguel Medina graduated schools. Driving exercises took place in the Ricote Valley, while shooting practice was conducted in Pliego and Yéchar (Mula). Theory lessons were held at the Casino of Archena, and the storage depot for spare parts was located in the Joaquín Gómez & Brothers fruit and preserves warehouse.

Before any Soviet tanks arrived at Archena, Colonel Sánchez-Paredes ordered the transfer of outdated French Renault FT-17 light tanks and Schneider CA1 heavy tanks, some armoured vehicles and even makeshift armoured cars to the base. The first Spanish trainees were recruited in early October 1936 when Sánchez-Paredes travelled to Madrid and Barcelona to select lorry, bus and taxi drivers who would be trained to operate the tanks and armoured vehicles expected from the Soviet Union. These recruits had to be approved by their respective trade unions.

The first shipment of T-26s, along with Soviet instructors, arrived at Cartagena on 12 October 1936. The tanks were immediately transported by rail to Alguazas and then onwards by road to Archena. The Soviet tank commanders and drivers came

On 16 October 1936, the first Republican tank company was formed, consisting of 15 machines and a select group of Soviet instructors and specialists (in soft caps), with the most advanced Republican trainees (in sidecaps) being assigned as gunners. The unit was led by Captain Pavel Arman. (Author's Collection)

from the best tank units of the Red Army, including the Volodarsky Mechanized Brigade, the 4th Separate Mechanized Brigade and the 1st Mechanized Corps from the Belarusian and Leningrad military districts. These instructors were chosen for their expertise, extensive military experience and political training. Before being deployed to Spain, they underwent additional training in Moscow, where they studied the technical, political and tactical conditions specific to the Spanish conflict and received practical recommendations.

The Soviet instructors began training the recruits immediately upon arrival at Archena. The first group of Republican tankers received only seven days of drill instead of the planned 15, however, as they were urgently called on to assist in the defence of Madrid. The first crews were trained in small groups of 4–5 tanks rather than at the company level. The only combat formations the Spanish tankers mastered were a march column and a deployed line formation for open combat.

On 16 October, the first tank company was formed, consisting of 15 tanks and a select group of Soviet instructors and specialists. Captain Pavel Arman led the company, with the most advanced Republican trainees being assigned as gunners. While the first trainees were sent into combat, training continued with numerous challenges, including language barriers, insufficient fuel supplies and a lack of technical knowledge among the Spanish crews. Taxi and bus drivers lacked the skills to adjust engine valves, so the Soviet instructors often acted as repair teams. Despite these difficulties, Spanish trainees were rarely punished for accidents. They 'were free to handle the tanks however they wanted' and were trained to operate them at high engine speeds.

Soviet instructors also faced the challenge of training tank crews that were largely composed of Communists; Socialists and Anarchists were excluded, limiting the pool of ideal trainees. To minimize wear on the tanks, training was initially conducted using stationary vehicles, thus depriving recruits of simulated combat experience. Nonetheless, the Spanish trainees showed 'great aptitude', quickly mastering stationary firing.

Unloading ammunition for the T-26 mod. 1935's 45mm 20K main gun. Only the simplest service duties were carried out by the Spanish tank crews themselves, while mechanical maintenance work was performed for an extended period by Soviet instructors. (BDH/BNE/CC BY 4.0)

Trainees were divided into specialized companies: drivers, turret commanders, tank commanders and mechanics. Each tank company consisted of 50 personnel. A Soviet advisor, typically a lieutenant, was assigned to each company commander, with additional support from two commanders and 3–4 junior instructors. Soviet mechanics and turret commanders also served as instructors for relevant courses. The language barrier made learning technical details and adhering to a strict schedule even more challenging. Tactical, theoretical and gunnery methodology lessons for officers were delivered in French by Colonel Semyon M. Krivoshein, with his deputy being Captain Arman. The tactical training of Spanish officers was rated as very poor, however, with reports stating that it was 'non-existent', and gunnery theory was completely new to them.

SEMYON KRIVOSHEIN

Semyon Moiseevich Krivoshein was born on 28 November 1899, into a Jewish family. After completing high school in 1917, he joined the 1st Red Cavalry Army under the legendary Semyon M. Budyonny. After the end of the Russian Civil War in 1923, Krivoshein was sent to the prestigious Military Academy 'M.V. Frunze' where he graduated, later holding the rank of major in charge of a mechanized regiment in 1933. In 1936, he volunteered to fight in Spain, where, in November and December of that year, he commanded the tank forces of the Republican troops during the battle of Madrid.

In January 1937, Krivoshein was recalled to the Soviet Union and promoted to Kombrig (brigade commander). In the summer of 1938, he led his brigade in the battle of Lake Khasan and participated in the occupation of Eastern Poland in September 1939. He also served during the Winter War against Finland (1939–40), earning promotion for his service. Within two years, he advanced from regimental commander to commander of armoured forces in the Baltic Special Military District and was promoted to major general in 1940, following the introduction of general ranks in the Red Army. After the German invasion of the Soviet Union in June 1941, Krivoshein received the highest awards for his role in the battle of Kursk in July–August 1943.

Later, Krivoshein took command of the 1st Mechanized Krasnograder Corps and led it during Operation *Bagration*, advancing his troops to Poland. By the end of the Great Patriotic War in May 1945, Krivoshein's corps was part of the 1st Belorussian Front under Marshal Georgy K. Zhukov in the battle of Berlin. He succeeded in breaking through German positions at the Seelow Heights and reached the Reichstag building in Berlin, for which he was awarded the title 'Hero of the Soviet Union'. It is also highly likely that his troops were involved in ending the flight of SS-Brigadeführer Joachim Ziegler, his German opponent during the Spanish Civil War.

Krivoshein commanded his corps until 1946, after which he taught at the Military Academy 'M.V. Frunze'. After Stalin's death on 5 March 1953, Krivoshein reached the end of his career, devoting himself after his retirement in May that year to writing his memoirs. He died on 16 September 1978 in Moscow at the age of 79.

With the arrival of a second batch of T-26s in early December 1936, the need for training intensified, especially as the new armoured brigade under Kombrig Dmitrii G. Pavlov's command was being formed. The brigade was to be divided into two battalions, with 60 per cent of its personnel consisting of Soviet crews and officers, while the remaining 40 per cent were Spanish or International Brigade members specifically trained for the role. By December 1936, the number of Soviet tankers in Spain was estimated to be about 250, but this number began to decline thereafter.

The staffing issue worsened in March 1937 when the armed cruiser *Cabo Santo Tomé* and the cargo ship *Darro* arrived from the Soviet Union on 6 and 8 March respectively, bringing 60 and 40 new T-26s between them – nearly as many as had been supplied since the beginning of Soviet involvement in the conflict. Many Soviet officers held unfavourable views of the Spanish tank crews, leading to plans to recruit tankers from the better-regarded International Brigades. These foreign volunteers were sent to Soviet tank schools in Gorky, and the first contingent returned to Spain in time for the Brunete campaign in the summer of 1937. Field-combat losses were sometimes replenished by using ordinary drivers or riflemen who were thrust into tanks to serve as gunners. During the 4–5km journey to the battlefield, they were hastily taught how to load shells and distinguish between armour-piercing and high-explosive rounds.

Combat revealed a significant gap in the training of tank crews regarding terrain orientation and map reading, often causing tanks to wander the battlefield throughout

A section of T-26 mod. 1935s prepare to enter combat. Kombrig Pavlov's tank brigade played a key role in the battle of Jarama by delaying the Nationalist advance with counter-attacks, buying time for the arrival of Republican reserves. (BDH/BNE/CC BY 4.0)

the night and only reach their positions by dawn. Despite many T-26s being equipped with radios, these were rarely used in combat. No training was provided for radio operation, and fine-tuning of the equipment often failed due to vibrations. After the first battles, the frames and antennas were cut off, and radios were made inoperative.

Once the T-26s were deployed in combat, it became clear that the main issue was not just tank-crew training, but the lack of coordination between tanks and infantry before and during missions. The Republicans could not afford to pull tank companies out of the front lines for such training, and Soviet advisor units were reluctant to spend precious engine hours on joint drills with the Spanish infantry. Additionally, as tank companies rarely worked with the same infantry units for more than a few days, there was no accumulated combat experience.

While training was essential to prepare the combatants for battle, field maintenance of the T-26s was equally critical to keep the force operational, and this was a major challenge. The tanks required intermediate overhauls at district workshops after 150 engine hours and a factory overhaul after 600 hours. Poor-quality fuel led to engine carbonization, fouled spark plugs and other issues that could immobilize the tanks. Tracks and track pins wore out after 800km, side clutches became worn and the powertrain was gradually misaligned from hard cross-country travel. The primary lessons learned from the autumn 1936 fighting focused on the technical issues that had to be addressed to keep the tanks in combat-ready condition.

To reduce wear on the T-26s, both sides turned to using commercial lorries to move them between battles, but the unreliability of the Soviet tanks, combined with inadequate maintenance by the poorly trained Spanish crews, resulted in abnormally high breakdown rates. This forced the Soviets to shift some of their experienced tank commanders to driver roles in an attempt to keep the tanks operational. This had a negative impact on combat effectiveness, however, as the more experienced Soviet tankers were no longer able to command the tanks and direct the gunners from the isolated driver's position.

Despite these technical and tactical challenges, Soviet and Spanish tank crews displayed immense bravery, a fact that was even acknowledged by the enemy.

This bravery often led to increased casualties among both personnel and equipment, however.

By October 1937, there was no longer a need to send more Soviet tank crews to Spain, as there were now a sufficient number of locally trained personnel for the tank units. According to Russian archives, approximately 350 military personnel of various ranks and technical roles passed through the Archena base during 1936–39, with most serving six-month tours, though some extended their service to up to a year.

NATIONALISTS AND GERMAN PERSONNEL

Similar to the Republicans, the Nationalists required extensive tank training, which was provided by the Germans. On 8 October 1936, a group of 267 German volunteers arrived in Spain, disembarking at Sevilla. Two days later, after several railway transfers, they began arriving in Cáceres. These volunteers, recruited from Panzer-Regiment 6 (3. Panzer-Division), were tasked with a mission described as being of 'some significance and high secrecy', though it was not disclosed that this mission would take place in war-torn Spain. These men were officially discharged from their German Army units while serving abroad to avoid revealing Germany's involvement in the Spanish Civil War. To maintain the ruse, they were to pose as a group of German tourists visiting Spain.

Upon entering Spain, the German tank group, known as Panzergruppe Drohne and led by Oberst Wilhelm Ritter von Thoma, settled on an estate about 15km from Cáceres, along the road to Mérida. The estate, which included two castles, was owned by the Viscount of Roda. After the military coup, the Viscount had ceded the estate to the Nationalist authorities for their use throughout the war.

Officers of Panzergruppe Drohne at Cubas de la Sagra. Front row, left to right: Hauptmann Joachim Ziegler, Oberst Wilhelm Ritter von Thoma, Hauptmann Peter Jansa. Second row, left to right: Oberleutnant Ernst Bothe, Oberleutnant Gerhard Willing, Hauptmann Eberhard Ostmann von der Leye. (Author's Collection)

The primary mission of the Germans was to train Spanish soldiers in the operation of PzKpfw I, using the tactical lessons they had learned in Germany. By November, an additional 37 men, 28 3.7cm PaK anti-tank guns and 21 new PzKpfw I Ausf B tanks arrived at the Cáceres base. At the same time, Panzergruppe Drohne's headquarters was moved to Cubas de la Sagra, a town closer to the front, where a training school, workshop and logistics base were established.

The German instructors taught the Spanish how to handle tanks – driving, technique, tactics and more – while also emphasizing other key disciplines essential for modern, multi-faceted warfare. At this stage, however, Oberst von Thoma found the Spanish trainees to be 'quick to learn and quick to forget'. The special training provided by the Germans also included the handling and use of flamethrowers and anti-tank guns, such as the Italian 47mm Cannone da 47/32 anti-tank gun. Drivers were trained to operate special vehicles, including heavy lorries for transport and Protze light artillery tractors for towing anti-tank guns. Courses were also held for master armourers, engine mechanics and other specialists.

Once the training was completed, Spanish trainees took possession of their first armoured fighting vehicles. The newly formed tank units were placed under the administrative umbrella of the Spanish *Regimiento de Infantería Argel 27* (Infantry Regiment Argel 27), which was organized as a tank battalion. This unit was commanded by Major José Pujales Carrasco, a former instructor at the Infantry Central Gunnery School, who would later be promoted to lieutenant colonel. The Spanish unit mirrored the structure of the German tank units, with a headquarters, two tank companies, a transport unit, a workshop and an anti-tank company. While the German instructors were officially in Spain to provide training only, they occasionally rotated to the front to offer further technical advice to the Spanish, engaging briefly in direct combat operations, such as those on the Madrid front in November 1936. Their combat involvement was much less significant than that of the Soviet advisors, however.

A German tank driver exits through the side hatch of a PzKpfw I Ausf A. While Panzergruppe Drohne personnel officially provided training and technical assistance, they also drove tanks between battles and, on occasion, even engaged in direct combat. (Author's Collection)

JOACHIM ZIEGLER

Joachim Ziegler was born in Hanau on 19 October 1904. After completing his school education, he joined the Reichswehr's Reiter-Regiment 15 in April 1923. By 1935, he had achieved the rank of *Hauptmann* in the 7. Kompanie, Panzer-Regiment 6. Shortly thereafter, he volunteered for Panzergruppe Drohne, commanding the 1. Panzer-Kompanie from November 1936 to March 1938. For his participation in the Spanish Civil War, he was awarded the *Spanienkreuz* (Spanish Cross).

In early 1939, Ziegler served as an adjutant and captain in the 3. Panzer-Brigade. On 23 September 1939, he was awarded the *Eiserne Kreuz 2. Klasse* (Iron Cross 2nd Class), and on 28 June 1940, he received the *Eiserne Kreuz 1. Klasse* (Iron Cross 1st Class).

On 14 March 1943, he was promoted to *Oberst* and served as a staff officer in the XXXXII. Armeekorps. Soon after, he was invited to take up a command position in the Waffen-SS. From 20 June 1943, Ziegler served as the chief of staff of the III. SS-Panzerkorps. In November 1943, he was granted permission to wear a Waffen-SS uniform for the duration of his assignment.

Following the death of SS-Gruppenführer Fritz von Scholz on 28 July 1944, Ziegler was given command of the 11. SS-Freiwilligen-Panzergrenadier-Division 'Nordland'. Its core consisted of Scandinavian recruits—particularly Danish and Norwegian volunteers. Ziegler adapted to his new role so effectively that by the end of August 1944 he accepted a permanent transfer to the *Waffen-SS*, though he remained a career *Heer* officer at heart.

From late October to December 1944, 'Nordland' remained in the Courland Pocket, and by early December its strength had fallen to just 9,000 men. In January 1945, the division was ordered to the Baltic port of Libau for evacuation by sea. Ziegler personally led counter-attacks near Libau, stabilizing a Soviet breakthrough, and in February he spearheaded the relief of the fortress of Arnswalde.

During the Battle of Berlin in April–May 1945, Ziegler delayed sending 'Nordland' to support the 9. Armee at the Seelow Heights by 24 hours, and instead positioned the division around Buckow, contrary to orders to deploy further south. His actions undermined the LVI. Panzerkorps' defence of the Oder front. His independent decision to withdraw westward ultimately brought his troops into Berlin, where they were surrounded by Soviet forces.

Ziegler considered the defense of Berlin both hopeless and pointless, particularly for the many non-German volunteers under his command. He sought to preserve their lives and attempted to disengage them from the front to surrender to American and British forces. During the battle of Berlin in April–May 1945, 'Nordland' was positioned south-east of the city and to the east of Tempelhof Airport. On 25 April, Ziegler was relieved of his command and replaced by SS-Brigadeführer Gustav Krukenberg. While attempting to break out of the encircled city with 'Nordland' personnel in the Brunnenstrasse near Humboldthain Park, he was wounded, and died on 2 May 1945.

In early 1937, the German instructors were tasked with the testing of captured T-26s and training Spanish crews to operate them. This proved challenging, as there were no operational manuals for the Soviet tanks. While the T-26's 20K main gun was familiar to the Germans – because the Rheinmetall company had sold the over-barrelled 3.7cm PaK to the Soviet Union – driving techniques and maintenance procedures had to be learned from scratch. Despite these challenges, the Nationalists managed to put an experimental platoon of T-26s into service by 13 February 1937.

In February 1938, when the Nationalist Tank Battalion became part of *La Legión* (the Spanish Legion) and was renamed the *Bandera de Carros de Combate de la Legión*, a new tank school was established in Casarrubuelos to train legionnaires in the handling and operation of armoured vehicles. The pool of trainees declined both in number and quality, however: personnel who were unsuitable for the Spanish Legion infantry battalions were often sent to the tank battalion, creating the

A section of PzKpfw I approaching Peñacastillo. Combat revealed significant shortcomings in tank-crew training, particularly in terrain orientation and map reading, which often resulted in individual crews becoming lost during operations. (Author's Collection)

impression that assignment to the tank units was a form of punishment. This was shocking to the Germans, as the Wehrmacht selected its tank crews from the best available manpower.

Moreover, because trained officers were frequently reassigned to other posts, basic officer courses had to be repeated continually, leaving little opportunity for advanced training. The tank school at Cubas de la Sagra continued to operate, but by now, its students were limited to officers, non-commissioned officers and soldiers from other units who voluntarily transferred to tank operations. By April 1938, just two months after the reorganization, only four students were training as drivers and gunners for the PzKpfw I, with an equal number being trained for Soviet tanks.

By the end of 1938, the number of German tank personnel in Spain had decreased to just 108, rendering the position of Tank Inspector, held by Oberst von Thoma, largely ceremonial. Despite this, Thoma continued to influence Nationalist tank operations, issuing several protests regarding what he saw as inadequate training for tank operators at the Casarrubuelos Tank School. He also criticized the misuse of tanks by Spanish crews, who sometimes fought on difficult terrain and were forced to cover long distances between combat positions, despite the Nationalists using heavy trucks to transport tanks when and where necessary. (This practice, which helped preserve the tanks' lifespan, was also adopted by the Spanish Army after the war.) While inadequate tank maintenance was unquestionably a more serious issue for the Republicans, the Nationalists also faced challenges, which the Germans highlighted.

Nevertheless, despite some disagreements between the German and Spanish forces, the *Panzertruppen* were instrumental in building the Nationalist tank force. Between 1 October 1936 and 31 March 1938, Oberst von Thoma's group trained 612 tank-crew members, including officers – 467 for the PzKpfw I and 145 for the T-26. In total, the Nationalist forces, including truck drivers, anti-tank gun crews and support personnel, numbered around 6,200.

THE COMBAT ENVIRONMENT

Despite the extensive efforts made by both German and Soviet advisors, neither group succeeded in fully preparing Spanish tank crews for prolonged tank operations under the specific operational conditions experienced in Spain, which proved to be exceptionally challenging. During the summer months, the blistering heat pushed temperatures up to 50°C, baking the ground and drying up nearly every waterway, leaving soldiers to suffer from intense thirst. The extreme heat inside the tanks, combined with the presence of powder gases and the stress of battle, left the tank crews physically and mentally exhausted.

As mucous membranes dried out rapidly, each crew member required at least 5 litres of water per day. Regular water was often insufficient to quench their thirst, however, so tank crews carried siphons of carbonated water, along with beer and a mixture of carbonated water and red wine. Owing to local conditions, it was impossible to prepare hot meals during or after battle, so the crews subsisted on canned food.

According to post-combat reports from Soviet tank crews, after a full day of fighting lasting 9–12 hours, the first 30–45 minutes were filled with heightened energy, but fatigue quickly set in. It became necessary to summon all of one's willpower to move from the spot and begin repair work on the tanks. Many times, T-26 crews rested for 3–4 hours after battle, either sitting or reclining inside their tanks, as they could not leave due to the lack of infantry support. The remainder of the time was spent maintaining the equipment.

Soviet sources report that after ten days of continuous tank fighting, the first signs of severe exhaustion began to appear: heightened nervousness, dulled hearing and widespread body pain. After 20 days of relentless combat, mental disorders, including delusions and hallucinations, began to emerge. A few days of rest were no longer sufficient to recover; a prolonged period of rest in a completely calm environment was necessary to restore the tankers' strength.

A photograph from the Lérida front showing a Republican T-26 mod. 1935 during the later stages of the Spanish Civil War, when most tank crews were of Spanish origin. (BNE/CC BY 4.0)

HOMECOMING

The German tank personnel who returned home after the Spanish Civil War were highly valued for their practical combat experience. Their time in Spain, where they were involved in both training and direct combat, provided invaluable lessons in tactics, coordination and the use of armoured vehicles. Upon their return, many German officers were entrusted with key roles in shaping the future of the *Panzerwaffe*. Some were appointed as instructors at the *Panzertruppenschule* (Armoured Troops School) in Wünsdorf, where they shared their hard-earned knowledge with the next generation of tank officers. Others were given leadership positions in various Panzer divisions. For example, Oberst von Thoma was promoted to commander of the 2. Panzer-Division's Panzer-Regiment 3.

In stark contrast, the fate of the Soviet tank personnel who participated in the Spanish Civil War was far less favourable. While many were appreciated for their contributions and some were decorated for their service, the political climate in the Soviet Union during the late 1930s was marked by suspicion and paranoia. Stalin's purges targeted many military leaders, including those who had gained significant experience abroad.

Paul Arman, who returned to the Soviet Union in January 1937, was initially entrusted with command of the 5th Mechanized Brigade. Owing to the political climate and the purges, however, he was arrested and imprisoned for two years. He was later reinstated and given command of armoured formations, including the 122nd Tank Brigade, only to be killed in combat by a sniper on the Leningrad Front on 7 August 1943. One of the most tragic cases was Dmitrii Pavlov, a highly regarded officer who earned the nickname 'the Soviet Guderian' for his expertise in armoured warfare. Despite his strategic acumen, Pavlov's career was ultimately ruined by the Soviet purges. In the immediate aftermath of the German invasion of the Soviet Union in June 1941, he was accused of 'negligence' for failing to prevent the German advance – a charge that led to his execution on 22 July.

Parade of the Legion Condor after the conclusion of the Spanish Civil War, held in Berlin on 6 June 1939. Soldiers in the second row, wearing characteristic black berets, represent Panzergruppe Drohne. (Author's Collection)

THE STRATEGIC SITUATION

The interwar period was the time for a debate on tank warfare, with the tactic of using small groups of tanks for close infantry support being criticized as outdated, in contrast to the concept of massed tank formations. There was also no consensus among advocates of armoured forces on whether large mechanized formations should be used to achieve breakthroughs during offensive operations, or held back until infantry, supported by tanks and artillery, had achieved the breakthrough, after which tanks would be deployed in the exploitation phase. This lack of tactical clarity led to the development of several different types of tanks for specific roles: slower tanks intended to support infantry divisions and faster or cruiser tanks designed for cavalry and deep-exploitation roles.

The Spanish Republican Army was free from such strategic dilemmas, however, as by the mid-1930s it had only two tank regiments: the *Regimiento de Carro* (1st Tank Regiment) in Madrid and the 2nd Tank Regiment in Saragossa, both largely equipped with World War I-era French Renault FTs, which were at best suitable for infantry support. When the Spanish Civil War broke out on 17 July 1936, most of the troops in the 1st Tank Regiment sided with the Republicans, while the 2nd Tank Regiment supported the Nationalists. The small armoured force was almost equally divided between the opposing forces: the 1st Tank Regiment's nine Renault FTs and four Schneider CA1s equipped the Republican side, while 2nd Tank Regiment's six FTs and two CA1s were in the hands of the Nationalists.

The Spanish landscape presented an often hostile environment for mechanized operations. Dominating the interior of the Iberian Peninsula was the Meseta Central,

By November 1933, when a large tank parade was held in Leningrad, the Red Army had already been supplied with nearly 2,500 T-26s in both twin- and single-turret variants. At this point, the Red Army possessed the world's largest tank force. (Author's Collection)

a vast high plateau that stretched across much of central Spain. While the region featured open flatlands that, in theory, were conducive to armoured movement, these were frequently interrupted by rolling hills, isolated ridges and poorly developed infrastructure. The limited road network, most of it unpaved and in poor condition during the 1930s, significantly hindered sustained tank operations.

In stark contrast, Spain's numerous mountain ranges severely restricted the movement of armoured vehicles. The Pyrenees in the north, and the Sistema Central and Sierra Morena ranges in the centre and south, formed formidable natural barriers. These mountainous areas featured steep inclines, narrow passes and rocky surfaces that proved impassable or hazardous for the light and underpowered tanks.

Urban environments posed an entirely different set of difficulties. Cities like Madrid, Teruel and Brunete – all key battlegrounds during the conflict – offered extremely limited manoeuvring space for armoured vehicles. Tanks operating in these areas were vulnerable to ambushes and concentrated anti-tank defences that included the use of Molotov cocktails and hand grenades. Somewhat more favourable conditions were found in coastal regions and river valleys, particularly in Andalusia and along the Ebro River. These areas featured relatively open terrain, fewer elevation changes and better access to road and rail networks. Even in these areas, however, terrain fragmentation and limited logistical support often hindered sustained offensive momentum.

Seasonal variations further complicated the use of armoured forces. In autumn and winter, heavy rains turned dirt roads and fields into quagmires, frequently bogging down or immobilizing light armoured vehicles. During the summer

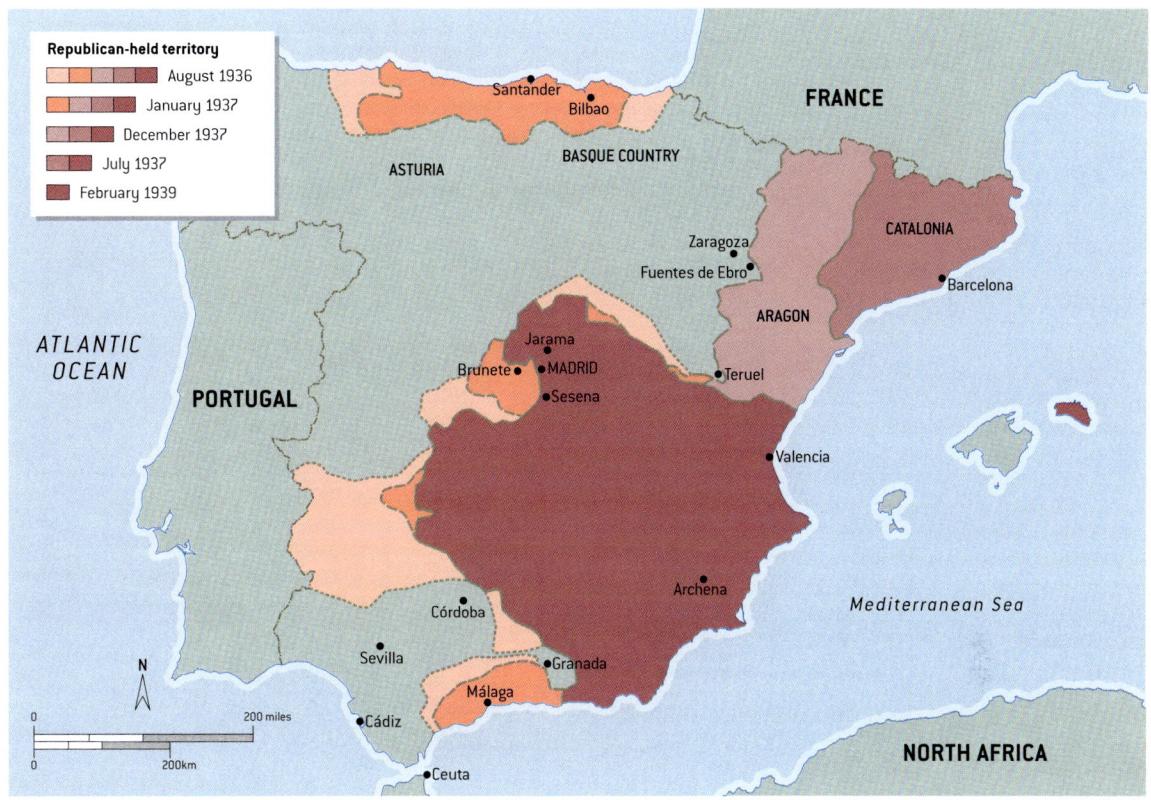

Republican-held territory

- August 1936
- January 1937
- December 1937
- July 1937
- February 1939

This map shows the progress of the Spanish Civil War, 1936–39.

months, extreme heat, dust and dry conditions placed a heavy strain on engines and air filters, reducing vehicle reliability and increasing the burden on maintenance crews. Visibility was also degraded by dust clouds, making command and control more difficult.

Despite the challenging terrain, tanks were still regarded as a potentially decisive form of weaponry. As a result, the Republican armoured force underwent rapid and significant expansion, largely enabled by direct support from the Soviet Union. Between 12 October 1936 and 13 March 1938, the Soviets delivered approximately 281 T-26s – widely considered the most effective armoured fighting vehicle of the conflict – and 50 BT fast tanks. While this was a notable contribution, it is important to remember that the tanks arrived in several shipments, and the fronts upon which they were deployed were widely separated. As a result, the Republicans rarely fielded more than 70–80 tanks at once, except on special occasions. Nevertheless, the sizeable presence of Soviet-origin armoured vehicles was enough to enable the formation of the *Brigada Blindada* (1st Armoured Brigade) as early as November 1936.

The Soviet Union supported the Republican side primarily because of an ideological alignment with left-wing forces, viewing the Spanish Civil War as an opportunity to combat fascism and promote the spread of communism in Europe. While ideological motives were at the forefront of Soviet support for the Second Spanish Republic, however, military considerations were also significant, particularly in terms of testing strategies and warfare.

By the mid-1930s, the Red Army had developed a coherent operational theory known as the 'deep battle', which called for the use of large motorized forces to penetrate the full depth of the enemy's defences. This concept had been established in the Red Army's Provisional Field Regulations of 1929 (PU-29), further refined by Marshal Tukhachevsky in PU-33 and codified in PU-36. These regulations were only general guidelines for motorized operations, however, and did not anticipate the specific challenges that tank units would encounter in combat. The Spanish Civil War provided an opportunity to address these issues in real combat conditions and develop relevant tactical recommendations. The advocates of the 'deep battle' concept did not, however, foresee that before they could learn from the Spanish experience, Stalin would begin purging the military leadership, starting with the arrest of Tukhachevsky and other senior officers. This removal of the advocates for armoured warfare in the Red Army was mirrored in 1938 by a sweeping purge of the tank-design bureaus, which resulted in the loss of key design teams, including those responsible for developing the T-26 used in Spain.

Similar to the Soviets, German involvement in the Spanish Civil War was driven by ideological motives as part of a broader strategy to support fascist regimes in Europe, particularly in the fight against communists, whom they viewed as a major threat. Additionally, Germany aimed to establish a counter-balance to France in Spain, which was seen as a threat to German ambitions in Europe. In addition to political reasons, the Spanish Civil War was expected to serve as a testing ground for new weapons, particularly for the Luftwaffe and, to a lesser extent, the newly formed *Panzerwaffe*. Although the *Panzerwaffe* had already committed to the offensive use of tanks in the mid-1930s, it needed to test both its equipment and tactical concepts in real combat conditions. It must be remembered, however, that at this stage, German tank capabilities were still limited both in terms of quantity and quality. As a result, the *Panzerwaffe* decided to deploy only 122 PzKpfw Is to Spain, delivered in several shipments, which were sufficient to establish just one tank battalion based on Panzergruppe Drohne, a German-staffed battalion-sized tank-training unit, which was mirrored by the *Batallón de Carros de Combate* (1st National Tank Battalion).

German tanks armed with machine guns could be effective against enemy infantry but were not suited for tank-vs-tank combat, which was viewed, however, as not the critical feature for the tanks of the mid-1930s, which were perceived to be infantry-support weapons. According to German analyses conducted in the 1930s, a battalion of 100 light tanks deployed on a 500m-wide front could easily break through an infantry division despite sustaining about 50 per cent losses – even if each defending anti-tank gun was credited with a kill for each round fired. Such a threat was considered to be a minor problem, however, because tanks were highly mobile and therefore hard to hit. It was believed that the PzKpfw I's armour was needed only to prevent penetration by armour-piercing bullets fired by machine guns – the weapons that killed infantry mobility during World War I and therefore had to be neutralized in a future conflict.

The true battlefield picture, just one month into the Spanish Civil War, revealed that German tactical analyses were far from accurate. The Germans had underestimated the effectiveness of well-organized anti-tank defences and the impact

of gun-armed Soviet tanks, which proved to be deadly opponents of light tanks and tankettes. These unforeseen challenges forced the Germans to adjust their tactics, and their tanks began to avoid direct confrontations with Soviet tanks, unless they could achieve numerical superiority and engage at very close range.

While German tanks did contribute to the success of the Nationalist forces in Spain, their role was not decisive. The Germans did, however, draw conclusions about the need to improve their basic anti-tank weapons and accelerate production of newer, better-armed and -armoured tanks. The first batch of the new PzKpfw III medium tank, armed with a 3.7cm KwK 26 L/45 main gun, was manufactured in 1936. Despite this early effort to improve tank firepower, by September 1939 only 87 of these tanks were combat-ready, demonstrating the slow pace of mass production and the challenges faced by the German industry in equipping its forces with the necessary tank models. At the same time, development of the PzKpfw IV medium tank, initially intended as an infantry-support tank armed with a short-barrelled 7.5cm KwK 40 L/48 main gun, also faced difficulties. By 1940, however, those models were already in mass production, ahead of the new Soviet models such as the T-34 medium tank and KV-1 heavy tank. This gave the Germans the opportunity to implement thorough training for tank crews, later deployed during the invasions of France and the Low Countries. This technical and tactical development, to some extent initiated by experience gained during the Spanish Civil War, ultimately provided the *Panzerwaffe* with a significant advantage over the Red Army's tank forces in 1941, when Nazi Germany invaded the Soviet Union.

By October 1936, German industry had produced 1,160 PzKpfw I Ausf As, followed by 403 PzKpfw I Ausf Bs. Hitler's generals believed this sizeable force was sufficient to break through even well-defended positions, especially when supported by motorized infantry and air power. (Author's Collection)

COMBAT

OPERATIONS, LATE 1936

The Nationalist forces began their push towards Madrid, where the Republican government was based, in August 1936. By late October, the Nationalists had captured several towns, forming the first defensive line surrounding the Spanish capital. On 28 October, Republican Prime Minister Francisco L. Caballero decided to launch a counter-offensive to halt the Nationalist advance towards Madrid.

On 29 October, the Soviet T-26s saw their first combat action when a force of 15, led by Captain Arman, encountered an advance guard detachment of General Francisco Franco's Nationalist forces at Seseña, about 30km south of Madrid. Initially, the T-26s managed to penetrate the Nationalist lines, but soon three were disabled by mines, and the rest lost contact with the supporting infantry. Another T-26 was damaged and immobilized by an Italian howitzer, and after 40 minutes of returning fire, the stricken tank was eventually knocked out by a field gun.

Despite these losses, the surviving T-26s pushed into Seseña, targeting Nationalist positions of opportunity. The lack of infantry support made them vulnerable to counter-attacks by Nationalist forces. One tank was destroyed by improvised petrol bombs, later known as 'Molotov cocktails'. The remaining tanks broke out of the town and launched a raid in the Nationalist rear, where they destroyed several artillery pieces. During this action, the Soviet tanks encountered three Italian CV 33/35 tankettes. One was destroyed at close range by tank fire, and another was pushed into

a ditch and overturned by the much larger T-26s. Before returning to the Republican lines, the T-26s destroyed many enemy lorries.

As Captain Arman's T-26s were engaged with the Italian tankettes, German PzKpfw Is joined the front at Santa Cruz del Retamar and Méntrida. The 1st Panzer Company of the National Tank Battalion experienced its baptism of fire on 1 November, providing support to Colonel Delgado Serrano's column during the occupation of Villamantilla, Villanueva de Perales and Brunete.

To contain the Nationalist advance, the Republican command launched a counter-attack on their right flank, deploying 35 T-26s, 20 gun-armed armoured vehicles and ten machine-gun-armed armoured cars. This armoured task force, led by Colonel Krivoshein, attacked the Nationalist forces on 3 November. They failed to break through, however, as the Soviet tanks came under intense artillery fire that destroyed two T-26s. A second Republican attack also failed. The next day, Krivoshein's formation, now including Captain Arman's company, launched another attack. Despite their efforts, the Nationalist troops occupied Leganés and Getafe in the suburbs of Madrid, advancing past the Villaverde–Orcasitas railway station. The Nationalist occupation of Getafe was supported by the 2nd Panzer Company. Further north, the 1st Panzer Company aided the Asensio column in capturing Alcorcón and the Cuatro Vientos airfield, where one tank was lost.

On 5 November, Arman's group lost three T-26s during a counter-attack on Villaviciosa de Odón, struck by anti-tank fire from the Castejón troop column. Krivoshein's group then retreated to Ocaña and later to Belmonte, where they were reinforced by two tanks and 13 BA-6 armoured cars from Archena.

On 6 November, the Nationalist columns approached Casa de Campo, a hilly and heavily wooded park on the western perimeter of Madrid, near the university campus. The following day, all available Nationalist tanks and tankettes were involved in an attack. The 1st Panzer Company was tasked with assaulting the military radio station and Casa de Campo but was thwarted by a Republican counter-attack by the 3rd Mixed Brigade, supported by Arman's T-26s. Meanwhile, the 2nd Panzer Company supported the Barrón column's attack on Carabanchel Bajo, though with minimal success. The Nationalist assault continued throughout the following week, with the 1st Panzer Company supporting Lieutenant Colonel Siró F. Alonso's column in an attack on the Lucero district, while the 2nd Panzer Company assisted the Barrón column in an attempt to cross the New Bridge over the Manzanares River.

The fighting peaked on 15 November, when German tanks attempted to attack in the area of the New Bridge but failed to cross it due to Republican fire, losing three tanks in the process. Owing to increasing pressure and the risk of being overrun, the Republican defenders finally blew up the bridge. Some reports suggest that two PzKpfw Is managed to cross just before the bridge's destruction but were isolated and destroyed. Later that same day, another attempt was made to cross the Manzanares River from the Casa de Campo area. The PzKpfw Is charged across, machine-gunning Republican trenches, but were stopped by the muddy riverbed and steep riverbanks. Most failed to reach the opposite riverbank, resulting in many being disabled or destroyed.

Despite these losses, the crossing was eventually made, and infantry from the Delgado Serrano column reached the university campus, occupying the stadium and the School of Architecture. While the PzKpfw Is fought around Casa de Campo and the university campus, Krivoshein's T-26s were engaged near Cerro Rojo. The Soviet tanks were confined to a narrow road due to steep hillsides, and two were destroyed by German 3.7cm anti-tank guns deployed near the summit.

Fighting in the suburbs continued for the next two weeks, with the Nationalist focus shifting to the left flank of the university campus penetration. The Asensio column was tasked with widening the gap and capturing the Moncloa Palace. All available Nationalist armour was involved, including two PzKpfw I companies and eight Italian tankettes, but no breakthrough occurred, as they were halted by anti-tank guns.

Throughout November, Krivoshein's T-26s continued to support the defence of Madrid. Each company typically supported an infantry battalion, although the terrain was not ideal for tank operations, and the tactical gains were minimal. By the end of the month, a few Soviet tanks were engaged in the narrow alleys of the university campus, where they proved to be vulnerable to Nationalist anti-tank fire.

A final tank engagement in the Madrid suburbs occurred on 25 November, when the Barrón column made a final attempt to capture the Cuartel del Infante Don Juan barracks and, via Plaza de la Moncloa, enter the streets of Madrid. Once again, anti-tank guns halted the PzKpfw I assault, and one of the Italian tankettes was disabled at the corner of Calle Moret and Plaza de la Moncloa. After a month of Nationalist attacks, the direct assault on Madrid was suspended, though not abandoned, as the capture of the capital remained the central objective of the war.

The first encounter between PzKpfw Is and Soviet T-26s around Madrid was frustrating for both sides. The Germans lost 15 tanks destroyed and 30 damaged, with 28 crew members killed and 118 wounded – most of them of Spanish origin – primarily due to anti-tank fire. The Republicans lost 16 T-26s, with 36 others damaged, though some were later repaired. Tank-vs-tank duels were rare, as both sides primarily used armoured vehicles to support infantry, but even these rare engagements demonstrated that the PzKpfw I was no match for the T-26.

Despite heavy losses, fighting around Madrid, particularly in the Pozuelo de Alarcón sector and along the road to La Coruña, continued until January 1937. By this time, both sides had deployed reinforcements, as their initial tank forces had been severely depleted by battlefield casualties and mechanical wear and tear.

OPPOSITE

This map shows the Nationalist attempt to storm Madrid in November 1936.

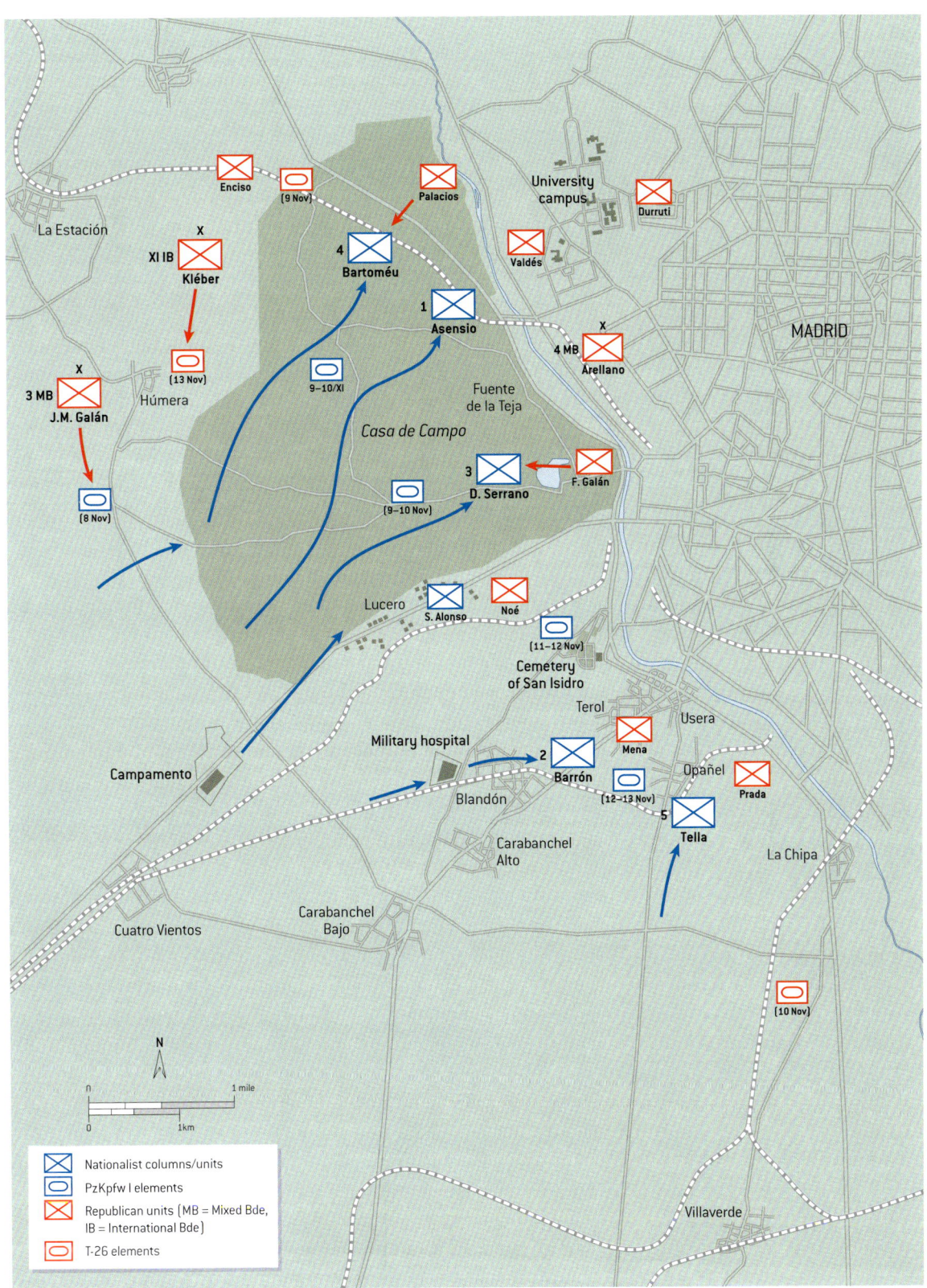

Enciso

(9 Nov)

La Estación

X
XI IB — Kléber

(13 Nov)

X
3 MB — J.M. Galán

Húmera

(8 Nov)

Palacios

4 Bartoméu

1 Asensio

9–10/XI

Casa de Campo

Fuente
de la Teja

University
campus

Durruti

Valdés

MADRID

X
4 MB — Árellano

3 D. Serrano

(9–10 Nov)

F. Galán

Lucero

S. Alonso

Noé

(11–12 Nov)

Cemetery
of San Isidro

Terol

Usera

Mena

Opañel

Prada

Campamento

Military hospital

2 Barrón

(12–13 Nov)

Blandón

Carabanchel
Alto

5 Tella

La Chipa

Carabanchel
Bajo

Cuatro Vientos

(10 Nov)

N

0   1 mile

0   1km

Nationalist columns/units

PzKpfw I elements

Republican units (MB = Mixed Bde,
IB = International Bde)

T-26 elements

Villaverde

Republican T-26s drove through Madrid in early November 1936. It must have been an incredible display of power for the people of Madrid to witness Captain Arman's tank unit, ready for battle against the enemy. (BDH/BNE)

OPERATIONS, JANUARY–FEBRUARY 1937

In early 1937, the newly formed Republican 1st Armoured Brigade, led by Kombrig Pavlov, was organized with a nominal strength of 96 T-26s, though it typically had fewer than 60 during the winter and spring fighting. The brigade was sent to the Madrid front aboard several trains that departed from Villacañas on 5 January. The next day, Pavlov's brigade clashed with Nationalist armour concentrated in the Estación de Pozuelo–Aravaca sector, setting fire to two PzKpfw Is from the newly formed 3rd Panzer Company, and damaging a third with an anti-tank gun. In return, one of the Nationalist anti-tank guns disabled a T-26, which was subsequently captured.

The Republicans continued their counter-attack on 11 January, with Kombrig Pavlov's tanks playing a prominent role, even managing to surround Las Rozas and Majadahonda. By the end of the day, however, the Republican infantry was unable to keep up with the tanks, and the situation in Seseña was repeated, though at a much higher cost. Over three days of fighting, Pavlov's brigade lost five tanks.

By mid-January, it became clear that PzKpfw Is, armed only with machine guns, could effectively damage T-26s only when using the special *Spitzgeschoss mit Kern Hart* (SmKH: 'pointed projectile with hard core') armour-piercing round capable of penetrating the Soviet tanks at ranges of about 120–150m. Once the Republican crews realized this, they avoided close-range combat and instead engaged at distances of up to 1km, ranges at which the T-26s' 45mm main guns remained effective, especially when stationary. Additionally, the T-26s' height allowed them to fire from above fences or from hollows, further enhancing their tactical performance.

To counter this, the National Tank Battalion deployed five German 3.7cm PaK towed anti-tank guns in each tank company. This solution was considered temporary, however, as the German guns were ineffective at ranges beyond 900m, whereas the T-26s could score hits at distances up to 3km. To address the situation,

Oberst von Thoma sent an urgent report to Berlin on 6 December, requesting that gun-armed tanks be deployed to Spain as quickly as possible. His request was denied.

After failing to capture Madrid by storm, the Nationalist forces attempted to encircle the city by crossing the Jarama River to the south-east and severing Madrid's communication with the temporary Republican capital of Valencia. The Nationalists' initial objectives were to capture the western bank of the river and the heights that overlooked it, and the National Tank Battalion was employed in this operation.

In response, the Republican *Ejército del Centro* (Central Army) sent Kombrig Pavlov's tank brigade (except for one company, which remained with the Madrid Army Corps) to the Arganda sector. The brigade's massed tank attacks, lacking organized infantry support, were the only force capable of resisting the Nationalist advance. While the Soviet forces did not break through the Nationalist lines, they delayed the enemy, allowing reinforcements to arrive and stabilize the front.

Tank fighting, including 26 PzKpfw Is newly arrived from Germany, continued until 27 February, resulting in heavy losses on both sides, mostly due to anti-tank guns. The overall outcome was unfavourable for the Republicans, who lost 14 T-26s (eight of which were captured by the Nationalists) and had another 20 tanks seriously damaged, compared to at least 11 PzKpfw Is lost by the Nationalists. Tank-vs-tank duels remained rare, but when they did occur, the German tanks had little chance of survival. The main lesson learned by PzKpfw I crews was that 'to overcome a T-26, another T-26 was needed'. The Nationalists' main challenge was acquiring more of them, which led to the Germans offering a cash reward for every captured T-26.

OPERATIONS, MARCH–JUNE 1937

In March 1937, the front shifted once again, this time to the north of Madrid, as an Italian offensive began at Guadalajara and Alcalá, opening on 8 March in foul weather. Although PzKpfw Is were not involved in this operation, a single battalion of CV 33/35 tankettes was allocated to spearhead the attack of four Italian divisions. These tankettes were, however, no match for the 60 T-26s deployed by Kombrig Pavlov's tank brigade.

On 13 March, near Trijueque, T-26s destroyed five CV 33/35s and damaged two more, without sustaining any losses. Five days later, the T-26s led a Republican counter-attack that routed several Italian units and secured the approaches to Guadalajara. Over the next few days, small groups of tanks attached to infantry brigades helped determine the outcome of the battle, which resulted in the destruction of the Italian *Corpo Truppo Volontarie* (Corps of Voluntary Troops). For the Soviet brigade, however, it was a Pyrrhic victory. Of the 72 Soviet tanks that participated in the battle, 28 were damaged or destroyed – hardly an improvement over earlier losses.

T-26 SIGHT

To aim the T-26's 45mm 20K main gun, the gunner used the PT-1 mod. 1932 tank periscopic sight. He had the choice of three reticles depending on the weapon being used. The reticle marked 'B' (*broniboyniy*) was for armour-piercing ammunition, 'O' (*oskolochniy*) for high explosive and 'P' (*pulemet*) for the machine gun. The reticles were conventional, having a centre crosshair aim point and a range scale, and below the crosshairs, a deflection scale in metres/kilometres.

The reticle shown here is the one used in conjunction with the periscopic sight for armour-piercing ammunition and was gradated to the maximum range of 3,600m; the high-explosive reticle had gradations out to 2,700m. As the periscopic sight was traversable for observation purposes, the gunner first had to lock the sight along the boresight of the gun. The range scale is above the crosshairs and is gradated in hundreds of metres (hectometres): 8 = 800m. The gunner employed a dial on the sight to adjust the elevation of the sight to compensate for range, with the selection indicated by the moving triangular indicator shown here in the 10 o'clock position for 600m.

PzKpfw I SIGHT

The PzKpfw I's twin 7.92mm MG 13 light machine guns were aimed using the Panzer Zielfernrohr 1 periscopic sight, which provided 2.5× magnification with a 28-degree field of view. The reticle consisted of a simple aiming chevron in the centre, allowing a well-trained gunner to fire at the maximum range of 800m. Effective range against infantry was around 500m, while the range against tanks using armour-piercing rounds was limited to 150m. Manufactured by Zeiss-Ikon at the Goerz plant in Zehlendorf, Berlin, these optics were designed to be mounted not only on tanks but also on a *Sockellafette*

(pedestal mount) or a *Kugellafette* (ball mount), which could be installed in fortified bunkers and fitted with machine guns.

To counter the better armed and -armoured T-26 tanks, the Germans had to use SmKH ammunition in their machine guns – an armour-piercing round with a steel jacket and a tungsten-carbide core. Even so, this cartridge could penetrate the T-26's armour only at ranges of up to about 150m, effectively forcing German infantry to engage Soviet tanks at very close distances.

PzKpfw Is advance through the Valley of Gordejuela, in the Las Encartaciones region of Vizcaya, en route to Valmaseda in April 1937. (BNE/CC BY 4.0)

Following the success at Guadalajara, the Republicans felt ready to take the initiative with an offensive. The first target was the Casa de Campo area near Madrid, with the aim of regaining control of the eastern bank of the Manzanares River. The attack began on 9 April, but the Nationalist positions held firm during the initial assault, allowing time for reinforcements to arrive. Among these were the 2nd Panzer Company, with 13 PzKpfw Is, as well as three captured ex-Republican T-26s. While the T-26s were used in static positions in the anti-tank role, the PzKpfw Is attempted to manoeuvre but were met with intense fire from the Republican T-26s, as well as artillery fire from Madrid and an armoured train positioned at the French Bridge.

By the end of April, the 2nd Panzer Company (excluding the Russian Tank Section) was ordered to move to the northern front to support the Nationalist offensive against Bilbao and Santander. A few days later, the next major Republican attack took place at Casa de Campo. More than 80 T-26s launched the attack against well-prepared anti-tank defences, with the Russian Tank Section contributing to halting the Republican assault. Between 5 and 12 May, 23 of the 84 active T-26s at Casa de Campo were damaged or destroyed.

The combat effectiveness of the captured T-26s led the Nationalists to begin modifying the PzKpfw Is with Italian 20mm Breda 20/65 mod.35 anti-aircraft guns, which were capable of penetrating the frontal armour of the T-26 at long range. The conversions were carried out at the Fábrica de Armas in Sevilla by late summer 1937, but only four modified PzKpfw I tanks were completed. The Germans were highly displeased with the modifications, calling the vehicles *Todespanzer* ('death tanks') due to an aperture in the turret front for the gun sight, which made the gunner vulnerable to small-arms fire. Ultimately, further conversions were halted, and by October 1937, Nationalist forces had captured ten intact T-26s and many more damaged ones that could be cannibalized for parts. These tanks were turned over to Oberst von Thoma's training centre for incorporation into the Nationalist units. Eventually, enough intact T-26s were captured that each PzKpfw I company was equipped with a single T-26 for fire support, and separate T-26 companies were gradually formed.

Combat medics from the 2nd Republican Battalion, named after Georgi M. Dimitrov, of the XVI International Brigade, evacuate wounded soldiers while being passed by Republican T-26 tanks during the battle of Brunete, July 1937. (BNE/ CC BY 4.0)

BRUNETE, JULY 1937

In the summer of 1937, one of the bloodiest battles of the Spanish Civil War took place near Brunete, a small town about 20km west of Madrid. The Republican offensive was initially planned as a pincer movement to encircle Nationalist forces west of Madrid, but the southern wing of the attack failed to launch, rendering the entire plan unfeasible.

On 5 July, 125,000 Republican troops, supported by 130 T-26s, launched an attack against 65,000 Nationalist troops, who initially had no tank support other than three ex-Republican T-26s, as all PzKpfw Is were concentrated in the north. Fortunately for the Nationalists, a supply of anti-tank guns had been distributed across all positions. The heaviest fighting occurred at the approach to the village of Villanueva de la Cañada, where a single anti-tank gun was credited with destroying 12 T-26s. Despite fierce resistance, the Republican forces managed to advance up to 20km into Nationalist lines. Their progress was cautious and lacking in initiative, however, which allowed the Nationalists to restore their defences.

By mid-July, the Nationalists decided to suspend their planned offensive against Santander and redirected the 4th and 5th Navarre brigades to Brunete. Along with these brigades, three PzKpfw I companies headed for Madrid. The Nationalist counter-offensive began on 18 July. Initially, the Nationalist divisions made only modest gains, facing intense resistance and continuous counter-attacks that hindered any significant progress. The 1st Panzer Company, which supported the Media Brigade, suffered the heaviest losses. To make up for the losses, 3.7cm anti-tank guns and captured T-26s were distributed across the Nationalist tank companies.

By the end of July, the battle of Brunete was over. The Republicans suffered nearly 15,000 dead or wounded, along with the loss of 21 T-26s destroyed and 26 more damaged. The Nationalists claimed to have captured 18 T-26s, six to ten of which were operational and could be incorporated into the National Tank Battalion. The Nationalists also sustained heavy losses, with an estimated 7,000 dead or wounded, as well as several PzKpfw Is destroyed.

OPERATIONS, AUGUST–NOVEMBER 1937

After Brunete, the Republicans never again managed to exploit their armoured units fully, losing the technical and tactical advantage they had once held. A report submitted to the Republican Defence Commissariat after the battle indicated that, out of 306 T-26s received from the Soviet Union, 80 had been destroyed by 1 September 1937, with another 17 requiring repairs. In total, 209 tanks remained operational: 123 on the Madrid front, 63 on the Aragon front and 23 on the southern front.

After the battle of Brunete, the 3rd Panzer Company headed north towards Alar del Rey to participate in the Nationalist offensive on Santander, which fell by the end of August. This loss, combined with the earlier capture of the heavily fortified city of Bilbao in June, created a significant and irreparable gap in the Republicans' Northern front. The Nationalists then continued their operations in Asturias, engaging the 1st and 2nd Panzer companies, along with the Soviet T-26 Tank Section, on the Aragón front. During this period, the newly formed 4th Panzer Company, equipped with PzKpfw Is, was also involved.

While T-26s made up the majority of the Republican tank force, the Soviets also delivered 50 BT-5s to Spain in mid-1937. These were similarly armoured and armed to the T-26 but much faster. They were assigned to the *Regimiento de Carros Pesados* (Heavy Tank Regiment). As the BT-5s were designed to exploit tactical breakthroughs, it was decided that they would be used to support an operation aimed at relieving pressure in Asturias, replacing a battalion of T-26s initially intended for the operation.

Nationalist Panzers enter the streets of captured Santander, passing Italian CV 33 tankettes. While both types were similar in size and armament, the German tanks were more versatile and technically reliable. (BNE/ CC BY 4.0)

On 13 October, the BT-5s were committed to a hastily planned attack on the town of Fuentes de Ebro. The operation ended in disaster, however, resulting in the loss of 19 of the 48 BT-5s engaged, with additional vehicles damaged and one-third of their crews killed or wounded. Following the failure at Fuentes de Ebro, it was decided to integrate the remaining BT-5s into the newly formed *División de Ingenios Blindados* (Division of Armoured Vehicles) in late October. This division consisted of the *Brigada de Carros de Combate* (Tank Brigade) with 124 T-26s, the *Brigada de Blindados* (Armoured Brigade), which was primarily equipped with armoured cars and just ten T-26s, and the Heavy Tank Regiment with the remaining 31 BT-5s.

At the same time, the organization of the National Tank Battalion was adjusted to accommodate the increasing number of captured T-26s. On 1 October, the National Tank Battalion was renamed the *Batallón de Carros de Combate* (1st Tank Battalion), which was organized into two groups, each with two PzKpfw I companies and one ex-Republican T-26 company. The 1st Group included the 1st and 2nd Panzer companies and the 3rd Soviet Company, while the 2nd Group included the 4th and 5th Panzer companies and the 6th Company equipped with Renault FT-17 tanks, which would be later replaced by T-26s. The battalion retained its anti-tank, workshop and transport companies. As the T-26-equipped company became the 3rd Company of the battalion, the one fighting in Asturias was designated the 4th Panzer Company. The 5th Panzer Company was newly formed with a batch of 30 PzKpfw Is received from Germany in two shipments – 18 to Vigo and 12 to Sevilla – in the second half of August.

The Puerta de Hierro-Hipódromo tram served as a grandstand for spectators during a military parade including this T-26 mod. 1935 at the sports facilities in Chamartín, held in the autumn of 1937 for the people of Madrid. (Author's Collection)

THE BATTLE FOR TERUEL, DECEMBER 1937–FEBRUARY 1938

The last major campaign involving Soviet tanks was the brutal fighting for Teruel, which took place between mid-December 1937 and the end of February 1938. The Republicans chose to attack the salient formed by the Nationalist front, which seemed vulnerable to encirclement despite several failed attempts previously. With a large volume of forces – including about 40,000 men, two T-26-equipped battalions and the remnants of the Heavy Tank Regiment – the Republicans believed success was guaranteed. In total, 104 tanks would be available for the operation, though by this point, nearly all Republican tanks had exceeded their expected mechanical lifespans.

The Republican breakthrough occurred during the early hours of 15 December, with infiltrations in both the northern and southern sectors following a heavy artillery bombardment. The Nationalist defenders, numbering fewer than 10,000 men, were overwhelmed by the Republican forces, allowing the latter to achieve some early local successes.

In response to the Republican offensive, General Franco ordered the deployment of the 62nd and 82nd divisions to the besieged city of Teruel. Along with these forces, the 2nd Group of the 1st Tank Battalion and T-26s from the 3rd Company of the 1st Group were also sent to the front. Although the Republicans maintained both quantitative and qualitative advantages, these were not effectively utilized. The Republican T-26s were primarily used in small units to support the slow-moving infantry, which often failed to keep pace with the tanks, making them easy targets for Nationalist anti-tank guns. The effectiveness of armoured attacks was further limited by the harsh weather conditions, among the most extreme of the war. Much of the battle was fought in temperatures as low as -20°C, in mountainous terrain and narrow village streets.

The months-long struggle for a few kilometres of ground finally ended on 22 February when the Nationalists recaptured Teruel and reclaimed all the territory they had lost to the Republicans in the previous month. Tank-vs-tank engagements were rare but the Republicans' BT-5 crews did claim a couple of Italian tankettes, while most of the tanks lost by the Republicans fell victim to Molotov cocktails during street fighting in urban areas. The technical challenges were so severe during the battle of Teruel that the 104 T-26s involved in the Republican offensive required repairs 586 times over the course of 65 days – approximately once every 11 days per tank.

The battle exhausted the Republicans' resources, leaving them unable to replace the men and equipment lost in combat. From the end of 1937, Republican tanks were relegated to secondary roles, supporting infantry or acting as mobile assault artillery. The *Ejército Popular de la Republica* (the renamed and reorganized People's Army of the Republic) typically assigned one tank battalion to each infantry division or army corps. The armoured brigades and armoured division were never used as cohesive fighting units, however, and the war devolved into a series of infantry battles.

OPERATIONS IN 1938

After the battle of Teruel, the Nationalist headquarters decided to launch an offensive towards the east, aiming to cut Republican-held territory in two. As preparations for this offensive began in February 1938, the 1st Tank Battalion was assigned to the Spanish Legion, becoming the *Bandera de Carros de Combate de la Legión*. Under this new structure, the two groups were renamed battalions, though the unit still maintained the same strength of six companies. The offensive in Aragón was to be supported by 67 PzKpfw Is, 29 T-26s, 52 Italian tankettes and approximately ten wheeled armoured vehicles. This force was intended to be used as a concentrated unit, rather than being spread out among infantry formations as it had been in the past.

The 'March to the Sea' began on 7 March 1938 and the initial stages of this offensive saw the most successful mechanized operations of the entire war. The Spanish Legion advanced with PzKpfw Is and T-26s, which helped break through Republican lines. The tanks were then followed by lorry-borne infantry battalions, rapidly advancing deep into Republican territory. Although it was not a classic Blitzkrieg, the operation's success was remarkable by the standards of the Spanish Civil War. For example, the army corps to which British volunteer Peter M.M. Kemp's battalion belonged advanced more than 50km on foot in a single day. Encounters with Republican tanks were rare, but when they did occur, they proved disastrous for the PzKpfw Is involved.

Finally, on 15 April, Republican-held territory was split in two, as were their armed forces, including the Division of Armoured Vehicles. The 1st Brigade, attached to the *Ejército del Este* (Eastern Army), included the 1st Tank Battalion, the 2nd Armoured Battalion, an independent armoured company and an infantry-support battalion. The 2nd Brigade, attached to the *Agrupación Autónoma del Ebro* (Ebro Autonomous Group), included the 3rd Tank Battalion, three armoured companies, one independent tank company and an infantry-support battalion.

On 24 July, Republican forces launched their final offensive across the Ebro River, one of the largest operations of the war. A total of 80,000 men, along with nearly all the armour available, were committed to the assault. Within 24 hours, the Republicans seized nearly 800 square kilometres of territory, but the Nationalists responded swiftly, sending a fresh division to help close the breach.

The Republicans suffered significant tank losses early in the campaign as the Nationalists managed to open the dams on the Ebro in the Pyrenees, causing flooding that swept away the bridges. As a result, only a small number of T-26s and a handful of artillery units were able to cross the Ebro. Most of the remaining Republican tanks were engaged near Gandesa. Despite initial gains, the Republican assault faltered due to Nationalist air and artillery superiority, and Colonel Juan Modesto, the Republican commander, was forced to order the *Ejército del Ebro* (Army of the Ebro) to go on the defensive.

The first Nationalist tank units arrived at the Ebro front on 29 July. Tank-vs-tank engagements were once again rare, but they did occur. On 2 August, for instance, the 5th Panzer Company, which had 'occupied the positions the enemy had used to strike with their tanks', forced four Republican tanks to retreat.

OVERLEAF

In March 1938, the 'March to the Sea' began, becoming the most successful National operation conducted by mechanized forces during the entire war. On 27 March, Nationalist forces reached the Cruz de Masatrigos and were forced to repel a strong counter-attack supported by Soviet tanks, four of which were captured. The Republican tanks claimed four Nationalist tanks destroyed and one abandoned. Here, a T-26 involved in the Republican counter-attack engages two PzKpfw Is at close range, reflecting the German tanks' limited capabilities at greater ranges.

A PzKpfw I and a T-26 of the Spanish Legion's 2nd Tank Battalion depart from Esplugues bound for Barcelona, during the final assault on the Spanish capital in January 1939. Photo taken by Francisco Martínez. (Author's Collection)

The battle of the Ebro continued until November, with armoured units from both sides playing a diminishing role in the later stages. By the end of the battle, it is estimated that 29 Nationalist tanks had been damaged or destroyed, including 11 T-26s. Of the Republican tanks that crossed the Ebro, 17 were lost, including six BT-5s, and another 18 were captured. When the battle concluded, the People's Army of the Republic ceased to exist as an organized military force. It should be noted, however, that both sides suffered significant losses during this extended confrontation.

THE INVASION OF CATALONIA, 1938–39

On 23 December 1938 the final offensive of the Spanish Civil War began, when Nationalist forces launched a massive invasion of Catalonia. The campaign swept through the region in the first two months of 1939. By this point, only Madrid and a few other strongholds remained under Republican control, but not for long. On 26 March, the Nationalists initiated a general offensive, occupying Madrid two days later. By 31 March, they controlled all Spanish territory. General Franco declared victory in a radio speech on 1 April, as the last of the Republican forces surrendered.

Out of 122 PzKpfw Is delivered to Spain during the war only 84 machines survived, which clearly proved that the first generation of German light tanks had little chance on the modern battlefield. Interestingly, by the end of the war, the Nationalists had captured a total of 178 Republican Soviet-supplied tanks, of which 98 T-26s were used in combat – quite sizeable number when compared to the 122 PzKpfw Is delivered by the Germans. The captured Soviet tanks were integrated alongside German and Italian light tanks and remained in service with the Nationalists until the mid-1950s, when they were replaced by US-made armoured fighting vehicles.

ANALYSIS

The Spanish Civil War is sometimes regarded as a testing ground for the ensuing World War II; in reality, however, its significance for armoured warfare was limited due to the small scale of the tank forces involved and their limited tactical objectives. Nevertheless, the fighting in Spain provided valuable lessons in the areas of technology, training and tactics, some of which were appreciated, while many were not.

Soviet tanks in Spain proved to be far superior to German tanks, but they never realized the potential that Red Army planners had envisaged due to their insufficient numbers, poor communication, hastily trained Spanish crews and a continual lack of maintenance support. This situation was further compounded by the perennial problem of ineffective integration of mechanized armour into the infantry's advance. The effectiveness of armoured operations was also limited by mountainous and rocky terrain, which differed significantly from the flat plains of Belarus and Ukraine. Nevertheless, the overall value of the Soviet tank contribution should not be understated. By most accounts, Soviet and Republican tank crews served bravely, and their presence provided the Republican forces with both practical and moral support. In just a few battles, they proved to be the difference – not necessarily between victory and defeat, but between defeat and disaster.

The most important lesson learned by the Red Army's from the Spanish Civil War was scepticism regarding the ability of independent tank groups to achieve breakthroughs against well-prepared defences. This led to the reorganization of the Red Army's tank forces in 1938–39, the intention being to spread tanks across rifle and cavalry divisions, thus limiting their role to direct support. This approach was reinforced by the disappointing performance of Red Army armoured brigades during the unopposed invasion of Poland in September 1939, as well as the catastrophic performance of tank units during the Winter War against Finland. In a November

1939 meeting of the Military Council, Soviet Defence Minister Marshal Kliment Y. Voroshilov advocated for the dismantling of the four tank corps, a proposal supported by the head of the ABTU (Directorate of Tank and Armoured Car Troops), Colonel-General Pavlov. This decision was influenced by Pavlov's experience in Spain and his fear of opposing Voroshilov and Stalin, which could have led to severe consequences.

The next organizational setback came in May and June 1940, when the Germans swept through France and the Low Countries. The stunning defeat of the highly regarded French Army by the German Panzer forces made it clear – even to Stalin – that the disbandment of the four tank corps had been a fundamental mistake. In June 1940, the Red Army commenced a drastic shift, initially forming nine massive mechanized corps, with plans to add another 21 starting in March 1941. The 1940 mechanized corps was a true corps in the Western sense of the term, composed of two tank divisions, a motorized division and corps troops, including an HQ and staff, a motorcycle regiment, communications and engineering battalions and an air-cooperation squadron. The formation of such large units was meant to prevent the exhaustion of the limited pool of even marginally competent officers, but the sheer size of these new formations simply underscored the acute shortage of trained mechanized unit commanders.

By June 1941, a total of 29 mechanized corps had been established, though not all were fully operational or combat-ready by the time the war with Germany began. Their backbone still consisted of T-26s, many of which were produced in the early 1930s. The new tank models, the T-34 and KV-1, while superior to their German counterparts, only began to enter service amid many technical issues. The organizational changes of 1938–40, combined with the lingering effects of Stalin's

Two T-26s of the Nationalist 1st Tank Battalion in Aragon, marked with tactical numbers identifying the 1st Company. The large crosses painted on top of the turrets were used as quick-recognition markings to distinguish Nationalist T-26s from Republican ones, thus helping to avoid 'friendly fire' from above. (BNE/CC BY 4.0)

purges – during which thousands of officers of all ranks were either executed or sent to labour camps – the poor training of average Red Army conscripts and the ongoing durability problems with older tank models, left the Red Army woefully unprepared for the Axis invasion of the Soviet Union that began on 22 June 1941.

German tanks operating in Spain were an even greater disappointment than their Soviet counterparts. They were practically defenceless against T-26s and anti-tank guns, poorly armoured and tactically mishandled, though they were mechanically more reliable than Soviet tanks. Despite these disadvantages, the Nationalists made the best of what they had in terms of their small tank force. They managed their resources better than the Republicans and made effective use not only of their own tanks but also of captured Soviet machines, a fact evident in the final outcome of the conflict. Still, they faced the same problems as the Republicans, including insufficient tank numbers, a lack of effective infantry support for tanks and an inefficient command-and-control system.

The experience in Spain prompted the Germans to reconsider their tank tactics and the combat usefulness of the PzKpfw I. Because these light tanks made up 35 per cent of the German Army's tank force at the outbreak of World War II, however, the Wehrmacht had little choice but to use them in combat during the early stages of the war, albeit in a completely different way than in Spain. From the very first day of the war, PzKpfw Is were deployed in large formations, supported by heavier tanks, motorized infantry, artillery and close air support. Drawing upon the combat experience gained in Poland, the Germans refined their tactics and battlefield command systems, which ultimately proved superior against French and British tanks in the spring of 1940.

Requetés of the San Miguel Tercio, a Carlist paramilitary formation, advancing in the La Serna area during the summer of 1937, supported by a PzKpfw I of the Nationalist tank battalion. (BNE/ CC BY 4.0)

AFTERMATH

On 12 August 1939, just a few months after the end of the Spanish Civil War, the Soviet–German Non-Aggression Pact was signed, which shocked governments around the world. A few days later, German Army PzKpfw Is and Red Army T-26s invaded Poland, this time as allies. Both parties regarded the pact as a tactical and temporary manoeuvre – Nazi Germany aimed to avoid a two-front war, while the Soviet Union sought to seize a great arc of territory to protect its western frontiers, including eastern Poland, eastern Finland, the Romanian provinces of northern Bukovina and Bessarabia and the Baltic states, and to prepare for a potential German invasion.

By mid-December 1940, Hitler requested plans for the invasion of the Soviet Union, codenamed Operation *Barbarossa*. At the outbreak of the operation, the German forces assigned to the invasion were equipped with 3,200 tanks. Although the majority were 2,068 PzKpfw IIIs and 500 PzKpfw IVs, there were also some PzKpfw Is and IIs. Approximately 150 of the former were assigned for reconnaissance duties in six (9., 12., 17., 18., 19. and 20.) of the 17 Panzer divisions set to be used against the Soviet Union. While it was clear that the combat value of the PzKpfw I was inadequate for modern warfare, the type remained in service due to tank-production difficulties faced by the Reich, which delayed the delivery of new tank models.

Additionally, around 150 examples of the PzKpfw I Ausf B were converted into pioneer tanks, equipped with explosive charge-dropping devices, and organized into *Panzer-Pionier-Kompanien*. Nearly 200 others were converted into light tank destroyers, known as the Panzerjäger I, which featured an open, lightly armoured superstructure and was armed with a Czech-built 4.7cm PaK(t) gun.

For the campaign in the Soviet Union, Panzer divisions were slightly modified in terms of armoured firepower. In fact, their strength was diluted to form more Panzer divisions. The German planners believed that concentrating several weaker Panzer

divisions together would achieve massive local superiority, which was crucial given the German awareness of the Red Army's advantage in tank numbers.

By mid-1941, the Red Army had around 24,000 armoured fighting vehicles under its command, approximately 35 per cent of which were T-26s. The number of technically operational T-26s in five border military districts amounted to only 3,100–3,200, however, as many were in need of major repairs – unsurprising considering that one-third of these tanks dated back to 1931–34. Considering all available types, however, including the brand-new T-34s and KV-1s, the Red Army still had three times as many combat-ready tanks as the Germans.

The start of Operation *Barbarossa* – designed to defeat the Red Army through large, enveloping manoeuvres close to the Soviet Union's western border, utilizing massive tank formations (*Panzergruppen*) that quickly broke through Soviet lines – achieved almost complete surprise. Generaloberst Erich K. Hoepner's Panzergruppe 4 played a key role in destroying the Red Army's 3rd and 12th Mechanized Corps before advancing through the Baltic states as the spearhead of Heeresgruppe *Mitte*'s push towards Leningrad, which was besieged on 8 September by Panzergruppen 2 and 3, leading Heeresgruppe *Mitte*'s advance, and which executed a spectacular encirclement east of Minsk, trapping about 30 Red Army divisions (including six mechanized corps) less than a week after the invasion began. These units were destroyed by German infantry divisions over the following three weeks, while German tanks advanced to trap another 21 Red Army divisions around Smolensk in mid-July. Meanwhile Generalfeldmarschall Paul Ludwig von Kleist's Panzergruppe 1, forming the main

German soldiers inspect an abandoned T-26 mod. 1931, a type unable to face *Panzerwaffe* tanks other than the PzKpfw I. Nevertheless, many of these twin-turret light tanks were used in 1941 for local Soviet counter-attacks against invading German forces, which typically ended in bloodbaths. (Author's Collection)

armoured strength of Heeresgruppe *Süd*, advanced deep into Ukraine, coming within 20km of Kiev by 11 July, after defeating desperate counter-attacks launched by the five mechanized corps of the Kiev Special Military District.

The Soviet tank force, led by the T-26s, launched numerous local counter-attacks to halt the enemy, but these operations were generally mishandled, often lacking proper infantry or artillery support. The Soviet forces even used obsolete, twin-turret T-26s in these counter-attacks, such as during a mid-July engagement near Zhlobin. A battalion of the 55th Tank Division, equipped with 36 T-26s (18 twin-turret models, including ten that were machine-gun-armed and eight that were gun-armed), reported the destruction of 17 enemy tanks while supporting the 117th Rifle Division. After heavy enemy tanks forced the T-26s to retreat, nine tanks managed to cross the Dnieper, but the remaining vehicles were lost, either destroyed or left on the battlefield.

The outcome of such engagements was disastrous for the T-26s, as their thin armour was vulnerable to all German tank and anti-tank guns at standard battle ranges. In contrast, the Soviet 45mm 20K main gun could only penetrate the up-armoured PzKpfw III Ausf H/J and PzKpfw IV Ausf E/F at point-blank range. Moreover, the three-man turrets of the PzKpfw III and IV allowed their commanders to focus on command duties, giving the German crews a distinct edge in tank-vs-tank engagements against most Red Army tanks. In the Soviet two-man turret, the commander had to divide his attention between commanding, gunnery and loading duties.

A T-34 (left) and a T-26 mod. 1938/39 abandoned in Ukraine during the summer of 1941. Inexperienced and poorly led Soviet crews were unable to capitalize fully on the superiority of the T-34's armament and armour over German tanks at this stage of the war, a situation that had already changed by 1942. (Author's Collection)

The only German tank type that proved completely useless was the PzKpfw I, which, in the opinion of Generaloberst Franz Halder, the German Army's chief of staff, was a burden for the units and should be sent to the rear to protect German territory and coastlines, as well as to serve for training purposes. A similar opinion was expressed by Major General Kirill S. Moskalenko, who stated that his 1st Motorized Anti-Tank Artillery Brigade drove off the enemy's light tanks with fire from 12.7mm DShK machine guns. By the end of August 1941, many PzKpfw Is were reported as total write-offs. Those that remained in front-line service until the end of 1941 were only used against entrenched infantry and other 'soft' targets. They were also tasked with towing lorries and other light (mostly wheeled) vehicles through the thick mud of the Russian autumn, or were relegated to rear-area duties, such as defending airfields or vital military installations in occupied enemy territory. By December 1941, attrition had wiped out the remaining PzKpfw Is, as no replacements had been issued to front-line units.

The exact number of T-26s lost during the first months of World War II is unknown, but by mid-July 1941, Soviet losses were staggering, totalling perhaps 5,700 armoured fighting vehicles. Many T-26 battalions lost up to 80–90 per cent of their initial tank strength. It should be noted, however, that many of these losses were the result of technical failures, as tanks with even minor damage were often abandoned, destroyed or burnt during retreats. Despite such losses, T-26s still made up the majority of the Red Army's tank force by the autumn of 1941. Many T-26s survived until the battle of Moscow (October 1941–January 1942), and the last major battles involving T-26s occurred during the Stalingrad campaign (July 1942–February 1943) and the Caucasus battles. One such engagement took place in December 1942, when the 207th Tank Brigade, equipped with 46 T-26s and six T-60 light tanks, engaged in intensive combat near Surkh-Digora, attempting to destroy a German tank battalion

T-26 mod. 1933 tanks from the 2nd Mechanized Corps, near Uman, Ukraine, in early August 1941, after engaging German tanks. The absence of heavy damage suggests these tanks may have been abandoned. The first month of the German invasion of the Soviet Union saw catastrophic losses for the Red Army, particularly among its tank forces. Many T-26 battalions were decimated, with some suffering losses as great as 80 per cent of their original strength. (Author's Collection)

During the long marches along the rugged, dirt roads of the Soviet Union in the summer of 1941, PzKpfw Is still in service like this Ausf B experienced many mechanical failures, particularly with the chassis. With workshop services not always readily available, due to the rapid advance of German forces, crews had to carry spare parts on tank hulls and carry out basic repairs on their own. (Author's Collection)

of the SS-Division 'Wiking'. Owing to poor organization, the brigade lost 37 T-26s and T-60s over two days, while knocking out 14 enemy tanks, ten of which were successfully evacuated by the Germans.

By 1943, T-26s were no longer in use on most sections of the Soviet–German front. They were retained primarily in rear units or sectors with stable fronts, such as Karelia and the Murmansk region, where they remained in service until the summer of 1944. By this time, the T-34 had taken over the role of the main battle tank in the Red Army's armoured force, capable of eliminating most German tank types.

By 1945 the last surviving T-26 tanks still served with the Soviet Far Eastern Military District, and although obsolete by Western standards, they earned an unlikely final chapter during the August campaign against Japanese-controlled Manchuria. During the drive on Mudanjiang, the 76th Tank Brigade pushed its T-26 battalion through terrain that heavier vehicles could barely enter. Where T-34s bogged down in marshes, the old light tanks slipped forward, scouting, seizing crossings and opening paths through country the Japanese believed impassable. Vulnerable in open battle, the T-26 nevertheless supported infantry assaults, shattered columns caught on the move and helped unravel the first defensive lines. In Manchuria, its weaknesses mattered less than its agility – and the limits of Japanese anti-tank weapons.

Fittingly, the T-26 became one of the few Soviet tanks to fight on what Japan regarded as its own 'internal territory'. On southern Sakhalin, machines of this veteran design accompanied the 214th Independent Tank Brigade's T-34s, closing out their service in fire, mud and victory.

BIBLIOGRAPHY

Balash, Yevgeny (2014). *Tanks of the Interwar Period*. Moscow: Tactical Press.

Baryatinsky, Mikhail (2008). *Soviet Tanks in Battle from T-26 to IS-2*. Moscow: Eksmo.

Candil, Anthony J. (2021). *Tank Combat in Spain*. Oxford: Casemate Publishers.

Franco, Lucas Molina & Garcia, Jose Mª Manrique (2008). *Blindados Alemanes en el Ejercito de Franco 1936–1939*. Valladolid: Galland Books.

Hooton, E.R. (2019). *Spain in Arms: A Military History of the Spanish Civil War 1936–1939*. Oxford: Casemate Publishers.

Isaev, Alexey (2012). *The Greatest Tank Battle of 1941*. Moscow: Eksmo.

Jentz, Thomas L. (2002). *Panzerkampfwagen I. Kleinetraktor to Auf. B.* Panzer Tracts 01-1: Old Heathfield.

Juntunen, Kim M. (1990). *U.S. Army Attaches and the Spanish Civil War 1936–39. The Gathering of Technical and Tactical Intelligence*. Author's thesis.

Kolomiets, Maxim (2007). *T-26 - The Hard Fate of the Light Tank*. Moscow: Eksmo.

Kolomiets, Maxim (2012). *Stalin's First Tank Victories*. Moscow: Eksmo.

Kolomiets, Maxim & Svirin, Mikhail (2007). *Light Tank T-26 1931–1941*. Strategy KM.

Kowalsky, Daniel (2020). *Stalin and the Spanish Civil War 1936–1939*. London: Bloomsbury Academic.

Ledwoch, Janusz (2003). *T-26 vol I/II/III*. Warszawa: Wydawnictwo Militaria.

Mata, José María; Molina, Lucas; Manrique, José María (2020). *German Military Vehicles in the Spanish Civil War*. Frontline Books, an imprint of Pen & Sword Books Ltd, Yorkshire – Philadelphia.

Mazarrosa, Javier de (1991). *Blindados en España*. Valladolid: Quiron Ediciones.

Perez, Artemio Mortera (2007). *Medios Blindados, Teatro de operaciones del Norte 1936–37 - Guerra Civil Española*. Valladolid: Alcaniz Fresnos.

Perez, Artemio Mortera (2009). *Los Medios Blindados en la Guerra Civil Española. Andalucía y Centro 36–39*. Valladolid: Alcaniz Fresnos.

Perez, Artemio Mortera (2011). *Los Medios Blindados en la Guerra Civil Española. Aragón Cataluña y Levante 36-39 1/2 parte*. Valladolid: Alcaniz Fresnos.

Spielberg, Walter J. (1974). *Die Panzer-Kampfwagen I und II und ihre Abarten*. Stuttgart: Motorbuch Verlag.

Thomas, Hugh (2001). *The Spanish Civil War*. New York, NY: The Modern Library.

MANUALS AND REGULATIONS

Tank manual   Panzerkampfwagen I (Sd.Kfz 101) – D-636, D-650.

Tank T-26 Service Manual, BT Armoured Tank Directorate of the RKKA, Voenizdat 1940.

Temporary Field Regulations of the RKKA 1936 (PU Z6). State Military Publishing House of the People's Commissariat of Defence of the USSR, Moscow, 1937.

INDEX

Page numbers in **bold** refer to illustrations and some caption locators are in brackets.